PSYCHOLOGICAL ASPECTS OF JATAKA STORIES

PSYCHOLOGICAL ASPECTS OF JATAKA STORIES

Exploring the Psychological Mysteries in Ancient Narrative

Ashin Sumanacara, PhD

Copyright © 2024 Ashin Sumanacara

All Rights Reserved.

No part of this book may be reproduced, distributed, or transmitted in any form or by any means, including electronic, digital, photographic, audiovisual, or any other information storage or retrieval system, whether currently known or developed in the future, without the prior written permission of the author. Brief quotations may be used for purposes of review, education, or non-commercial use, provided appropriate credit is given.

Library and Archives Canada Cataloguing in Publication

Psychological Aspects of Jataka Stories/Ashin Sumanacara

    Paperback Book ISBN 978-1-7782016-9-1

    Hardcover Book ISBN 978-1-7782016-8-4

    Electronic Book ISBN 978-1-7782016-7-7

Published by:

SUBHASHITA BOOKS

Laval, QC. Canada.

Cover Photo Credit:

The cover features a depiction of a Jataka story from the mural paintings in Ajanta Cave 1. This ancient artwork portrays a significant episode from the Buddha's past lives, reflecting the rich tradition of Buddhist storytelling.

In Dedication

To the monastic and lay communities, whose teachings and support have shaped this work.

TABLE OF CONTENTS

PREFACE i

PROLOGUE iii

INTRODUCTION v

CHAPTER ONE

DREAM: UNCONSCIOUS THOUGHT, DESIRES, AND CONFLICTS IN JATAKA STORIES

    Introduction 1

    Functionality of Dreams 2

    Significance of Dreams 5

    The Sixteen Dreams of King Pasenadi in the
    Mahasupina-jataka 6

    Dreams in Other Jataka Stories 26

    Conclusion 36

CHAPTER TWO

PATHOLOGICAL GRIEF: THE PSYCHOLOGICAL IMPACT OF LOSS IN JATAKA STORIES

    Introduction 43

    Pathological Responses to Grief 44

    Types of Pathological Grief 53

    Grief Treatment Process 60

    Other Grief Themes 67

Conflicts in the Portrayal of Grief in the Jataka
Stories   70

Conclusion   72

CHAPTER THREE
DESIRE: THE HUMAN DRIVE AND ITS CONSEQUENCES IN JATAKA STORIES

Introduction   79

Feeding   81

Fleeing   86

Fighting   88

Fornicating   93

General Desires from all Senses   98

Conclusion   102

CHAPTER FOUR
PSYCHOLOGICAL DISORDER: MENTAL HEALTH CHALLENGES IN JATAKA STORIES

Introduction   107

Attachment Disorder   109

Antisocial Personality Disorder (Psychopathy)   112

Antisocial Personality Disorder and Extreme
Violence   116

Narcissistic Personality Disorder and Humanistic
Therapy   118

Narcissistic Personality Disorder and Cognitive-
Behavioral Therapy   123

Enmeshment of Family Structures	125
Prolonged Grief Disorder	127
Sex and Love Addiction	132
Psychosis and Schizophrenia	135
Conclusion	137

CHAPTER FIVE
SEXUALITY: EXPLORING HUMAN RELATIONSHIPS AND IDENTITY IN JATAKA STORIES

Introduction	145
The Implication of Women's Wickedness in Jataka Stories	148
Homosexuality	171
Sexual Satisfaction	174
Conclusion	176

CHAPTER SIX
SUBSTANCE ABUSE: COPING MECHANISMS AND MORAL LSSONS IN JATAKA STORIES

Introduction	179
Consequences of Alcohol Addiction	181
Stigma of Alcoholism	194
Enabling Alcoholism	204
Conclusion	206

PREFACE

The Jataka stories are a captivating collection of Buddhist narratives that have resonated with readers for centuries. These tales explore not only moral teachings but also the complexities of the human psyche, offering unique insights into the human experience. This book presents a detailed examination of the psychological dimensions within these ancient stories, providing readers with an in-depth look at the layers of consciousness embedded in each narrative.

Each chapter of this book delves into specific themes such as dreams, grief, psychological disorders, desire, sexuality, and substance abuse, drawing connections between these universal human experiences and the Jataka stories. By doing so, the book aims to foster a deeper understanding of the psychological forces shaping human behavior, while also offering tools for emotional reflection and growth.

Written for scholars, students, and general readers alike, this book bridges academic rigor with accessible prose, making its exploration of Buddhist psychology applicable to a wide range of readers. Through its detailed analysis, the book offers a fresh perspective on the psychological aspects of these stories, providing timeless insights into the workings of the human mind.

In addition to its academic value, this work seeks to inspire personal introspection, inviting readers to consider how the timeless lessons of the Jataka stories can apply to their own lives. By intertwining ancient wisdom with modern psychological frameworks, the book aspires to enrich both intellectual understanding and emotional well-being. It is my hope that this exploration will spark thoughtful dialogue and deeper engagement with the rich legacy of Buddhist thought.

Ashin Sumanacara
PhD in Buddhist Studies (Mahidol)

PROLOGUE

The Jataka stories, deeply embedded in Buddhist teachings, extend far beyond moral guidance; they offer profound insights into human psychology and behavior. Despite their importance within Eastern traditions, these psychological dimensions remain underexplored in Western academic discourse. This gap presents a significant opportunity for further study, particularly within the field of psychoanalysis, where ancient wisdom and modern psychology can intersect.

This book addresses this gap by analyzing the Jataka tales through the lens of Buddhist and Western psychology, with a focus on psychoanalytic theory. The stories provide fertile ground for examining unconscious desires, emotional conflicts, and mental health, themes that resonate strongly with foundational concepts in Western psychology. By comparing these ancient narratives with modern psychoanalytic frameworks, this book uncovers both parallels and contrasts in the ways human psychology is understood across cultures.

Through this cross-cultural analysis, the book highlights the psychological depth of the Jataka stories and brings these dimensions into academic and public awareness. By doing so, it opens new avenues for dialogue between Eastern and Western perspectives, enriching our understanding of consciousness and emotional experience across time and tradition. Ultimately, this work contributes to the broader discourse on human psychology, providing fresh insights into both individual struggles and collective mental states, as captured through these ancient Buddhist narratives.

INTRODUCTION

The Jataka stories are a captivating collection of tales woven into the fabric of Buddhist literature. Originating from ancient records documenting the Buddha's pre-enlightenment experiences, these stories extend beyond traditional moral lessons, exploring the complexities of the human psyche. Through their psychological depth, the Jataka stories offer timeless insights into the human mind, inviting readers to delve into the intricate layers of each narrative.

In Psychological Aspects of Jataka Stories, readers will encounter a comprehensive examination of the psychological components within these tales, gaining a deeper appreciation of the diverse dimensions of the human psyche. This book explores themes such as dreams, grief, desire, psychological disorder, sexuality, and substance abuse, revealing profound psychological revelations within each narrative.

The Jataka stories provide a deep understanding of human desires, fears, and aspirations through the exploration of dreams. By utilizing vivid dream sequences and symbolism, these stories unlock the mysteries of the human psyche and reveal the layers of consciousness often obscured in daily life. Emphasizing the symbolic language of dreams, the Jataka tales encourage readers to uncover hidden meanings, offering a captivating glimpse into the unconscious mind and the psychological foundations of human existence.

The Jataka stories also offer a profound examination of the universal experience of grief and loss, providing insights into the emotional landscape of human bereavement. Acknowledging grief as a shared experience arising from various life circumstances—such as loss or change—these narratives explore emotional responses ranging from sadness and anger to guilt and anxiety. The Buddhist perspective on grief recognizes it as an essential part of the human experience, offering guidance and solace to those navigating its complexities. By contemplating grief and loss within the Jataka stories, readers gain a deeper understanding of sorrow and compassion.

Psychological disorders, extensively researched in both science and literature, are also explored in the Jataka stories. These narratives offer valuable insights into the complexities of the human mind, highlighting the nuances of psychological distress. Through the mental disorders portrayed in these tales, readers can foster empathy and understanding of the intricate psychological terrain that shapes human experience.

Desire, a central theme in Buddhist philosophy, plays a key role in the Jataka stories. According to Buddhism, desire is a root cause of human suffering and a major obstacle to enlightenment. By exploring desire, these narratives offer insights into the psychological mechanisms behind longing and attachment, promoting a deeper understanding of the complex nature of human desire.

The Jataka stories also delve into the interplay between sexuality and desire, offering a multifaceted view of human sexuality within cultural and spiritual contexts, including Buddhist teachings. Through these narratives, readers gain an understanding of the intersection between spirituality and sexuality, fostering insights into the psychological dimensions of love, attachment, and desire.

Additionally, the Jataka tales provide commentary on the effects of substance abuse and addiction, shedding light on the psychological layers of dependency. Substance abuse is a global issue, affecting individuals, families, and communities, making it essential to examine the psychological underpinnings of addiction. The stories offer perspectives on the causes and consequences of addiction, as well as potential paths to recovery and healing.

Psychological Aspects of Jataka stories offer a comprehensive analysis of these narratives, revealing the intricate layers of the human psyche. This book is an invaluable resource for academics, students, and professionals interested in understanding the complex psychological forces that shape human existence. By exploring themes such as dreams, grief, desire, mental health, sexuality, and addiction, readers will uncover profound insights into the workings of the human mind.

CHAPTER ONE

DREAM: UNCONSCIOUS THOUGHT, DESIRES, AND CONFLICTS IN JATAKA STORIES

Introduction

The study of consciousness has been a topic of perpetual contemplation, delving into the intricacies of thought, sensation, and awareness. For the purpose of this discussion, we will define consciousness as a state of responsiveness and awareness within one's environment (Blackmore & Troscianko, 2018). It is worth noting that various renowned scholars in psychology and philosophy offer diverse definitions of consciousness, all of which focus on the theme of environmental awareness and responsiveness (Nunn, 2009). This, in turn, makes the concept of consciousness intrinsically linked to the notion of the unconscious, as proposed by psychoanalyst Sigmund Freud.

The concept of the unconscious, as posited by Freud, is a subject of perennial fascination due to its profound and enigmatic nature. It represents the deepest stratum of the mind that remains beyond conscious awareness. Nonetheless, Freud underlines the pervasive influence of the unconscious on human behavior despite its concealed dimensions. In this regard, the idea of the "waking state" becomes significant as it suggests that the unconscious is accessible during sleep, offering a potential avenue to explore the mysteries of the unconscious mind through dreams.

With this backdrop, this chapter examines the sixteen dreams of King Pasenadi as documented in the Mahasupina-jataka (Ja 77) within the framework of Buddhist and contemporary Western dream theories. The initial segment will offer an overview of current dream theory within Western psychological science. Subsequently, the application of these concepts to the King's dreams will be explained, followed by an exploration of other dreams referenced in ten distinct jataka tales and their relationship to established dream theories.

Functionality of Dreams

The examination of dreams has played a crucial role in the development and formation of Freud's understanding of the mind. Throughout history, fields such as research, psychology, and therapy have utilized dreams as a tool to diagnose the underlying causes of psychological disorders. However, several studies have suggested that dreams may serve various other functions. Notably, scholars such as Carl Jung have addressed dream theory and its relation to the unconscious. In contrast to viewing dreams as manifestations of the unconscious, Jung focused on their functionality and usefulness (Jung, 1984). In his view, the mind operates as a self-regulating system that aims to protect and aid us.

Emotion Regulation

According to Fosshage's (1987; 1997) theory, dreams serve as a crucial regulatory tool for emotions and contribute to psychological structuring. Moreover, experimental studies suggest that dreams can have therapeutic benefits for individuals who have undergone trauma (Hartmann, 1998) and can facilitate coping mechanisms during wakefulness (Picchioni & Hicks, 2009). Contemporary research in the field of dreams suggests that the characters and interactions we experience in our dreams play a significant role in regulating our emotions in our waking life (Nielsen & Larra-Carrasco, 2007). Dreams possess an adaptive quality that has enabled us to survive and adapt to life's challenges (Moffitt et al., 1993; Kramer et al., 1976; Hartmann, 1996).

Memory Consolidation

Numerous studies have delved into the significance of dreams, concluding that they play a pivotal role in converting short-term memory into long-term memory (Schoch et al., 2018; Born & Wilhelm, 2012). This is further supported by the reactivation of memory encoding-related brain regions during slow-wave sleep in rats (Girardeau et al., 2017; Marshall & Born, 2007). While dreams are usually associated with rapid eye movement (REM) sleep rather than slow-wave sleep, there is still a debate among researchers as to whether dreams aid in memory consolidation. Stepping away from neurological data, the notion that dreams facilitate memory consolidation is corroborated by the consistent reflection of waking events in dreams (Schredl & Hofmann, 2003).

Insight into Psychological Problems

Freud, the renowned psychotherapist, posited that dreams could reveal hidden insights into the unconscious mind and its underlying issues (Freud, 1955). Furthermore, some therapists have incorporated dreams into their psychotherapy practices to augment the therapeutic experience. Greenberg and Pearlman (1978) conducted a study indicating that individuals who dreamt during psychotherapy were more likely to form profound emotional connections with the therapeutic process. This suggests that such dreams may stem from an attachment to the therapy itself rather than a genuine psychological ailment.

Modern psychology has developed a consensus theory of dreaming through empirical dream research. According to this theory, dreaming occurs when the brain is not receiving new environmental stimuli, but it can utilize its enhanced functionality to solve problems and stimulate creativity (Barrett, 2007). The majority of scientists agree that dreams have the ability to convey information from the unconscious to the conscious, particularly if the dream is remembered upon waking.

As we contemplate the nature of dreams and their place in our lives, it is common to wonder about their significance. Are they random images that our brains generate during sleep, or do they convey deeper meanings and messages? And if they do, who has the authority to decipher them? These complex questions have puzzled philosophers, scientists, and ordinary people alike for centuries, and they continue to spark lively debates and discussions to this day.

Significance of Dreams

Dream analysis involves deciphering the meaning behind our dreams' various elements, characters, and emotions. While it is an important tool for gaining insight into our subconscious, there has been debate surrounding the idea of creating "dream manuals" or "dream books" that offer universal interpretations of dreams. However, such books rely on two unproven assumptions: that dreams can predict the future (known as prophetic dreams) and that they are universally symbolic and carry the same meaning for everyone. As a result, this area remains complex and challenging for empirical scientists to study.

Despite any preconceptions, early scholars delved into the realm of dream interpretation and examined the literature to uncover shared interpretations of the symbols that commonly appear in dreams (Hall, 1953). The consensus of this approach revealed that a singular concept, such as a mother, could manifest as a variety of symbols for different individuals, ranging from a cow to a tree.

Dream interpretation is a complex practice that is further complicated by cultural differences in who is authorized to interpret dreams and the standardization of dream symbols. While this chapter focuses on the therapeutic benefits of accessing the unconscious through dream interpretation, the practice has been culturally and cognitively significant in early societies. To properly interpret dreams, there must be shared cultural assumptions between the interpreter and the dreamer.

In addition to the difficulty of standardizing the meanings of dream symbols, cultures differ significantly in terms of who has the authority to interpret dreams. Dream interpretation is discussed when accessing the unconscious for therapeutic purposes.

The Sixteen Dreams of King Pasenadi in the Mahasupina-jataka

King Pasenadi's sixteen dreams have been the focus of much attention, with most modern Buddhist scholars interpreting them as prophecies that have come to fruition in the present day. Unlike psychoanalytic approaches that emphasize the unconscious mind, these dreams are not seen as offering insight into the King's inner psyche. According to the Mahasupina-jataka (Ja 77), the Bodhisatta informed the King that the dreams were not related to his personal life, emotions, or mental state.

The story revolves around King Pasenadi, who was childhood friends with Bodhisatta. Troubled by the dreams, the King turned to his Brahmins for guidance. They, too, interpreted the dreams as ominous prophecies and recommended animal sacrifice as the only way to avert misfortune.

The King, terrified, spared no expense in constructing a grand sacrificial pit and purchasing the finest animals for sacrifice.

Studies have revealed that nightmares, especially those that seem to have a prophetic meaning, can cause more distress when awake than during the actual dream (Halliday, 1987). Despite the fact that such dreams may be unsettling and terrifying, the King may not necessarily experience fear while asleep. We will delve deeper into these dreams later on. Moreover, the King appears to have accepted the Brahmin's interpretation of the dream as factual and, as a result, takes significant measures to address the dreams. This highlights the cultural significance of dream interpretation, as discussed by Edgar (2002) since the King did not necessarily seek out the assistance of a psychological or dream expert.

Upon receiving a recommendation, she found unsatisfactory, Mallika, the King's wife, suggested seeking counsel from the Bodhisatta. In certain versions of the tale, a young and wise Brahmin implores the King to find a different solution to his dreams. Despite the Brahmin's efforts to explain that sacrificing one life does not ensure the safety of another, the King remains stubbornly unmoved. Frustrated, the Brahmin retreats to the garden. It is worth noting that while these characters all object to the King's response to the Brahmin's interpretation of his dream, they do not necessarily disagree with the interpretation itself. They all seem to believe that the Brahmin's interpretation is correct and that the dreams are a warning of impending trouble. The crux of the disagreement lies in the actions taken to address the dreams, which is a separate issue from dream interpretation (Kilborne, 1981).

Dream: Unconscious Thought, Desires, and Conflicts

In this story, the Bodhisatta appears before a young Brahmin in the garden, seemingly traveling through the air. The Bodhisatta takes a seat on the ceremonial stone and engages in a conversation with the young Brahmin. During their exchange, the wise Bodhisatta inquiries about the righteousness of the King's rule. The young Brahmin expresses dissatisfaction with the King's decision to sacrifice animals based on the advice of other Brahmins. He implores the Bodhisatta to explain to the King that this is not the solution to his dreams. The Bodhisatta agrees, and the young Brahmin brings the King to the garden. Once the King reveals his sixteen dreams to the Bodhisatta, the Bodhisatta assures him that there is no need to worry. The King is convinced and cancels the sacrifice, living a righteous life following the five precepts until the end of his days.

Contemporary analysis of the sixteen dreams implies that they hold prophetic significance. In order to soothe the King's concerns, the Bodhisatta provided an explanation that each dream foretells a future event. Additionally, he conveyed that these prophecies are the result of humankind's avarice and animosity. While the Bodhisatta's words provided solace to the King, they also indicated that these events would occur long after his reign had ended. It is worth noting that the Bodhisatta's interpretation differs greatly from that of the Brahmins.

Out of the King's sixteen dreams, ten involve animals. These animals often display unusual and deformed characteristics or engage in nonsensical and unnatural behaviors. Throughout history, different philosophical traditions have offered various interpretations of animals as dream symbols (Doidge, 2005; Platek, 2008). Notably, Sigmund Freud associated animals in dreams with symbols of genitalia, such as mice representing unconscious thoughts about pubic hair and snakes symbolizing a man's penis (Freud, 1955). While universal symbol meanings require further discussion, this chapter delves into the animal symbols in the King's dreams, which is in line with existing research on animal dream symbolism.

Apart from animal symbols, non-animal dream symbols have also been given attention (Shredl, 2013). However, in this animal dream, the focus lies on thoroughly scrutinizing the actions and behaviors of the actors and objects within the dream rather than solely on their inherent qualities (Roesler, 2018).

First Dream: Four Robust Oxen

In King Pasenadi's first dream, four sturdy oxen emerged from the cardinal directions—north, east, south, and west—appearing ready for combat before the monarch. However, they inexplicably retreated just as they were about to collide. Bodhisatta's interpretation of this dream foresees an era of moral decay and ecological instability, where human misbehavior disturbs the inherent balance of the planet. He likens the withdrawal of the bulls to the unfulfilled pledge of precipitation, underscoring how human avarice can disrupt the planet's ecological harmony (Ja 77).

Due to the lack of a universally agreed-upon interpretation of the symbolism of bulls throughout different civilizations, they often hold significant meaning as animal symbols in dreams (Milne, 2011). Typically, they are associated with traits such as stubbornness and resilience, leading many dream analysts to interpret their appearance as a representation of inner strength (Milne, 2011). Bodhisatta's perspective supports this idea, drawing a connection between bulls and the path of human growth.

Within the framework of Buddhism, the four oxen symbolize the worldly distractions and attachments hindering spiritual progression. Their varied directions emphasize the pervasive nature of desires and worldly entanglements, while their withdrawal points to the impermanence of such attachments, reflecting the Buddhist principle of transience.

According to psychological analysis, the four powerful oxen in a dream may symbolize various aspects of the dreamer's psyche that are vying for dominance and expression. The oxen's movements suggest a complex interplay of conflicting thoughts and emotions within the subconscious mind, and their sudden withdrawal may indicate a temporary suppression of internal conflicts. The bulls represent primal instincts and unconscious impulses, while the King figure represents the conscious ego trying to maintain control. The bulls' withdrawal reflects the operation of defense mechanisms, revealing the intricate dynamics between the conscious and unconscious mind.

Second Dream: Growing Plants Bearing Fruits

In the second dream, King Pasenadi dreams of small trees and shrubs, each standing no more than a foot or two tall, yet bearing fully grown fruit. According to Bodhisatta's interpretation, these events will occur after the king's time, symbolizing young women marrying early and bearing children, with the blooming trees representing their offspring and impending maternal roles (Ja 77; Kramer, 1987).

When viewed from a Buddhist perspective, the dream serves as a reminder of the interconnectedness of all living beings, highlighting the importance of cause and effect and the impermanence of life. The flourishing plants and their fruits symbolize the cyclical unfolding of karmic consequences, underscoring the significance of positive actions for a more meaningful life (Bodhi, 1994).

While the significance of tree symbolism in psychology has yet to be extensively explored, there have been documented instances of dream acts involving climbing or moving among trees (Hall, 1953). The depiction of thriving flora and their bountiful yield can be interpreted as a manifestation of the dreamer's unconscious desire for creative fulfillment and productivity. This imagery is suggestive of an innate urge for emotional gratification and self-expression, indicative of the dreamer's underlying aspirations and desires (Freud, 1955).

Third Dream: The Mother Cow Nourishes Herself with Her Calf's Milk

In the third dream, King Pasenadi dreams of a scenario that defies natural laws, where fully grown adult cows are shown sucking the milk of newborn calves. Bodhisatta interprets this dream as a warning of a future where respect and reverence towards parents and elders have deteriorated (Ja 77).

In this vision, elderly parents are forced to contribute to the household, relying on their adult children for support, much like the image of a fully grown cow drawing sustenance from a calf.

This dream reflects the interconnectivity of familial ties and the societal shift in values. As respect for elders diminishes, the dream underscores the importance of mutual respect and nurturing within families, as emphasized in Buddhist teachings. It serves as a reminder of the Buddhist precept of honoring one's parents and promoting harmony within the home.

Hall's work on dream symbols highlights the complexity of animal symbolism, emphasizing that interpretations often rely on one's personal associations with the symbols (Hall, 1953). Within the dream, the image of a mother cow drinking her own calf's milk can represent unconscious desires for emotional nourishment. This symbolism points to a lack of external emotional support, pushing individuals to seek internal sources of comfort and self-reliance.

Fourth Dream: Farmer Using Young Oxen for Transportation and Abandoning the Strong Ones

In the fourth dream, King Pasenadi dreams of fully grown work oxen struggling to carry a weighty load. The burden is then passed on to a group of younger and less experienced oxen, who are ultimately unable to move the weight, forcing the caravan to halt.

This scenario exemplifies a society's deviation from wisdom, where the focus shifts from experience to youthfulness, causing instability. Communities that prioritize juvenescence over expertise risk losing the direction and steadiness that seasoned individuals provide.

According to Bodhisatta's interpretation, this dream foretells a future decline in moral values. Government leaders will be driven by hatred, greed, and a lack of principles, choosing less experienced individuals over seasoned ones. Like the young oxen struggling to bear the load, these leaders will be unable to fulfill their responsibilities, resulting in national suffering and their eventual resignation (Ja 77; Bodhi, 1994).

From a psychological perspective, this dream may symbolize an internal struggle between relying on inexperienced aspects of one's life, represented by the young oxen, and neglecting the proven, reliable elements, akin to the strong oxen. It could also reflect a fear of change or resistance to adopting new methods despite current inefficiencies.

Interestingly, ancient religious and historical texts mention oxen as another animal dream symbol. Research on this symbol has focused less on the presence of oxen and more on their actions, which are crucial to understanding the symbol's meaning. For instance, oxen grazing has been interpreted as a symbol of trade success. This interpretation aligns with the Bodhisatta, who emphasized the animals' actions rather than their identity.

Fifth Dream: The Two-Headed Horse and the Divided Feast

In the fifth dream, King Pasenadi dreams of a curious vision—a horse with two heads eating separately from two different containers instead of sharing. The Bodhisatta provided an insightful analysis that placed the dream in a historical context where unqualified and avaricious rulers appointed equally corrupt officials to the judiciary. These judges, enticed by material wealth, tainted their verdicts by accepting bribes from both parties, thereby compromising the very essence of justice (Ja 77).

From a Buddhist perspective, the dream serves as a warning against the negative consequences of greed, corruption, and injustice. The two-headed horse consuming from two sources represents the duality of unethical behavior and the erosion of moral integrity. This dream emphasizes the importance of upholding fairness, ethical conduct, and truth in society.

Horses are a common recurring symbol in dreams, often associated with Freudian theories of unconscious sexual desires (Lewis, 2008; Van de Castle, 1983; 2012). The presence of a horse is typically interpreted as a phallic symbol (Hall, 1953).

According to psychoanalysis, dreams can reveal internal conflicts. The two heads of the horse may symbolize conflicting thoughts or desires, reflecting disharmony between different aspects of one's personality. Eating from separate sources without sharing could suggest an ongoing internal struggle or the need for balance and integration within the self.

Sixth Dream: People Instigate a Jackal to Urinate on a Cherished Golden Bowl

In the sixth dream, King Pasenadi dreams of a perplexing scene where people request an old jackal to relieve itself in a precious golden bowl. Bodhisatta's interpretation of this dream predicts the deterioration of moral values in future rulers, where the trust in elders is forsaken, and unqualified individuals are appointed to significant governmental positions (Ja 77).

From a Buddhist perspective, this dream serves as a symbol of the degradation of values, where personal integrity is compromised by societal pressures. It reflects the challenges of maintaining ethical standards in a culture driven by materialism and external approval. The jackal defiling the golden bowl underscores the clash between maintaining moral integrity and succumbing to societal expectations.

The ideal situation symbolizes the challenges that people face when trying to uphold their moral values, especially in a culture that prioritizes material possessions and external approval. This emphasizes the difficulties of maintaining personal integrity in the midst of societal pressures that could potentially lead individuals to betray their ethical beliefs. The story highlights the fine line between staying true to one's principles and giving in to societal expectations, demonstrating the intricacies of maintaining moral integrity in an environment that may not fully acknowledge or value such virtues.

From a psychoanalytic perspective, the image of coercing a jackal to defile a prized possession suggests self-destructive tendencies arising from unresolved psychological conflicts. This could represent subconscious urges leading to behaviors that undermine one's achievements or values, reflecting inner struggles between personal success and hidden desires (Freud, 1955).

Seventh Dream: The Crafty She-Jackal and the Spinning Threads

In the seventh dream, King Pasenadi dreams of a man spinning threads and keeping them near his legs, while a she-jackal stealthily tries to eat the threads without the man noticing. Bodhisatta interprets this dream as a sign of future moral corruption, particularly focusing on women's changing roles. He foresees women in the coming era engaging in intense desires for men, seeking sexual gratification, and neglecting their traditional domestic duties (Ja 77). Women, like the she-jackal gnawing at the threads, will deplete their husbands' resources.

From a Buddhist perspective, the dream scenario described can be interpreted as a reflection of the concepts of attachment and desire. The man's tireless weaving depicted in the dream may symbolize the devoted efforts and contributions one makes in one's relationships or home. Conversely, the woman's attempt to consume the threads may represent a fixation on material possessions or desires that contradict the principles of ethical conduct and integrity. This analysis aligns with Buddhist teachings that emphasize the importance of cultivating detachment from material possessions and desires in order to attain inner peace and enlightenment.

From a psychoanalytic viewpoint, the dream can be analyzed as a representation of the dreamer's subconscious tensions and desires. The act of spinning threads could symbolize the creation or preservation of something valuable or significant in the dreamer's life. The man's protective behavior towards these threads may reflect an unconscious need to safeguard personal creations or achievements. On the other hand, the wolf's covert attempts to devour the threads may signify hidden desires or anxieties that are undermining these accomplishments.

Eighth Dream: Neglected Small Pitchers Amidst an Overflowing Main Pitcher

In the eighth dream, King Pasenadi dreams of a scene where small pitchers are ignored while a main pitcher overflows. The dream depicts a grand palace gate with a generously filled pitcher surrounded by several empty pitchers. Crowds of people continually refill the overflowing main pitcher, neglecting the nearby empty ones.

According to Bodhisatta's interpretation, this dream symbolizes a future decline in both men and kings. The overflowing pitcher represents the king's demands for constant service, while the neglected pitchers signify the subjects and their families, whose needs are disregarded in favor of serving the king's desires (Ja 77).

Modern interpretations of dreams with abstract symbolism focus less on specific symbols. Although some studies have examined the significance of water in dreams (Hall, 1962), those who follow Freud's theories may view flowing water as having sexual connotations.

From a Buddhist perspective, dreams can serve as a powerful illustration of the dire repercussions that can result from misguided leadership and misplaced priorities. The emphasis on blindly serving corrupt leaders at the expense of one's own loved ones and community underscores the potential for immense suffering. This highlights the vital importance of virtuous leadership and cultivating a strong sense of communal responsibility within society. By doing so, we can pave the way for a more fair and equitable society rooted in the principles of compassion, wisdom, and ethical behavior.

From a psychoanalytic perspective, the overflowing main pitcher could symbolize a dominant figure or aspect of life receiving excessive attention, leaving other important needs unfulfilled. The empty pitchers represent neglected elements of the dreamer's life, suggesting unresolved psychological conflicts related to care and attention. This interpretation explores subconscious representations of favoritism or neglect, possibly reflecting early life experiences that influence present emotional dynamics.

Ninth Dream: The Tainted Lake and the Thirst of Beasts

In the ninth dream, King Pasenadi dreams of a serene pool nestled amidst lush banks, adorned with five distinct species of lotus flowers. Various creatures, both bipedal and quadrupedal, gather at the water's edge to quench their thirst. Interestingly, the center of the pool remains muddy, while the water surrounding the banks is crystal clear and inviting.

According to Bodhisatta's interpretation, this dream foretells a time when corruption among rulers and kings leads to the displacement of citizens. The center of the pool represents the corruption in the judiciary, while the clear edges symbolize the forced migration of people to the outskirts due to excessive taxes and bribes demanded by corrupt leaders (Ja 77).

From a Buddhist perspective, the dream highlights the destructive effects of selfish and corrupt leadership. The muddied center of the lake symbolizes the harmful influence of greed and lack of ethical governance, causing suffering and disruption in society. The clear water at the edges represents the desire for a simpler, more just way of life, free from the burdens of corrupt leadership. This reflects the Buddhist values of compassion, fairness, and the responsibility of rulers to care for their people.

Research suggests that dream animals are often drawn from one's daily experiences, whether encountered in person or through media (Shredl, 2013). Therefore, the creatures depicted in the dream are likely familiar to the king, regardless of Bodhisatta's interpretation.

From a psychoanalytic viewpoint, the polluted central lake could be a metaphor for inner turmoil caused by self-serving leadership. The pristine edges of the lake symbolize the dreamer's subconscious desire for solace, balance, and escape from oppressive circumstances. The dream may reflect concerns about power and the role of empathy and compassion in leadership, emphasizing the importance of ethical governance and care for the community.

Tenth Dream: The Pot of Unevenly Cooked Rice

In the tenth dream, King Pasenadi dreams of rice being prepared in a single pot, with some parts overcooked, some undercooked, and some perfectly cooked. The dream highlights the significance of water as a representation of life, interacting dynamically with the rice in diverse ways. Water's uneven distribution among the rice reflects the unevenness of life's nourishment and sustenance. In this context, rice represents the subconscious pursuit of spiritual fulfillment, which is backed by studies on dream symbolism and food representation (John, 2000). The Bodhisatta suggests that human tendencies towards greed stem from an inner void. However, he does not directly attribute these symbols to the king's unconscious desires, diverging from his interpretation of the remaining dreams.

From a Buddhist perspective, the dream highlights the impermanence and unpredictability of life. The erratic cooking of the rice symbolizes the karmic outcomes of one's actions, where individuals experience both favorable and unfavorable results. This aligns with the Buddhist teaching that life's dualities are interconnected and shaped by past deeds.

From a psychoanalytic viewpoint, the varying degrees of rice doneness represent different aspects of the dreamer's emotional state. Overcooked portions may reflect feelings of stress or overwhelm, while undercooked grains suggest areas of life that feel incomplete or unfulfilled. In contrast, perfectly cooked rice symbolizes a sense of balance and satisfaction, indicating the dreamer's desire to achieve harmony in their life.

Eleventh dream: The Foolish Trade of Sandalwood for Sour Buttermilk

In the eleventh dream, King Pasenadi dreams of a peculiar transaction where sandalwood, valued at 100,000 monetary units, is exchanged for sour and rancid buttermilk—an exchange that defies rationality. This peculiar trade symbolizes a distorted exchange of value, defying common sense and reflecting deeper issues of corruption and greed.

From a Buddhist perspective, this dream highlights the dangers of greed and the corruption of sacred teachings. Bodhisatta's interpretation emphasizes the risk of even monks succumbing to material desires, twisting the Enlightened One's teachings for personal gain. The exchange of sandalwood for buttermilk serves as a metaphor for the degradation of spiritual values, reminding practitioners to preserve the integrity of Buddhist doctrines and resist the temptation to profit from sacred knowledge (Ja 77).

From a psychoanalytic viewpoint, this dream may represent the unconscious desire to obtain external possessions as a way to fill internal voids. The irrational exchange of valuable sandalwood for worthless buttermilk could symbolize an attempt to mask emotional shortcomings or pursue quick fixes for deeper psychological needs. This dream suggests a potential inner conflict between material pursuits and the longing for meaningful fulfillment.

Twelfth dream: Sinking Dried Pumpkins

In the twelfth dream, King Pasenadi dreams of pumpkins, hollowed out and waterlogged, sinking beneath the water's surface. Bodhisatta's analysis of this dream revealed a future where inexperienced and unwise people hold positions of power and authority, usurping the place of knowledgeable and revered leaders (Ja 77). The laws they enforce are emblematic of the hollowness of their reign, much like the sinking pumpkins. While limited research exists on the symbolism of pumpkins in dreams, modern interpretations tend to focus on the paradoxical nature of something inherently hollow carrying significant weight, as noted by Hall (1953).

From a psychoanalytic viewpoint, the sinking pumpkins may symbolize feelings of insecurity or fear of failure. The dream could reflect an unconscious worry about losing control in challenging situations, revealing deeper anxieties about one's abilities to handle responsibilities or succeed under pressure.

Thirteenth Dream: A Massive Solid Rock Floating Above the Water's Surface

In the thirteenth dream, King Pasenadi dreams of massive rocks gliding effortlessly across the water's surface, defying natural laws and echoing the surreal nature of his previous visions. Bodhisatta's analysis aligns with the previous dream, illustrating the rise of unworthy leaders who float effortlessly on the water's surface, while the weighty rocks represent the sinking of honorable leaders. This dream signifies a decline in the appreciation and understanding of virtuous principles and wisdom (Ja 77).

From a Buddhist perspective, this dream symbolizes the challenge of upholding righteousness in a world dominated by unethical forces. The floating rocks represent misguided ideas and the rise of corrupt leaders, while the sinking of worthy leaders highlights the neglect of ethical values. This emphasizes the importance of maintaining unwavering ethical conduct and integrity, even when faced with adversity, aligning with Buddhist teachings on moral strength and perseverance.

Stones are a frequent occurrence in dreams and have been interpreted in various ways. According to Freudian theory, stones may symbolize phallic imagery, while others see them as a representation of infancy or teeth (Wilson, 1967).

From a psychoanalytic perspective, the floating rocks could symbolize an imbalance between appearance and reality. The effortless floating may suggest a superficial, yet unsustainable, rise to power or success, while the weight of the rocks indicates the eventual collapse of such false achievements. This dream may reflect subconscious fears of inadequacy or concerns about the lack of depth and substance in leadership or personal accomplishments.

Fourteenth dream: Frogs Consume Large Snakes

In the fourteenth dream, King Pasenadi dreams of tiny frogs successfully hunting and devouring large black snakes with ease, as though the snakes were insignificant prey. The interpretation of Bodhisatta suggests that intense desires and imbalanced power dynamics in marital relationships drive a society. Younger wives' dominance over their husbands highlights the complexities of passion-fueled unions and their potential consequences (Ja 77).

From a Buddhist perspective, this dream illustrates the complex interplay of attachment and desire in personal relationships. It highlights the importance of balance and mindfulness in fostering harmonious connections based on understanding and wisdom. The dominance of the frogs over the snakes emphasizes the need to approach relationships with mindfulness and ethical considerations, aligning with Buddhist teachings on cultivating healthy, balanced relationships.

From a psychoanalytic viewpoint, the frogs devouring the snakes could represent the power of the subconscious mind to overcome significant challenges. The image of the frogs dominating the larger snakes symbolizes the potential for smaller, hidden aspects of the self to take control or overpower seemingly dominant elements. This dream reflects inner conflicts between assertiveness and control, and the need for careful discernment in navigating these subconscious struggles.

Fifteenth Dream: A Crow Encircled by Golden Geese

In the fifteenth dream, King Pasenadi dreams of a crow indulging in the ten vices, surrounded by a flock of golden geese. According to the interpretation of the Bodhisatta, the crow symbolizes an upcoming, immoral King who seeks to establish a court that bolsters their self-centered tendencies. This misguided ruler distanced themselves from honorable advisors and faithful mentors, convinced that associations with unsavory characters would enhance their standing. As a result, such rulers embrace ignorance and dismiss the guidance of those who may offer differing viewpoints (Ja 77).

Birds have long been a subject of interest in the realm of dreams, with crows being of particular significance. They are often seen as symbols of freedom due to their ability to fly, as noted by Shredl (2013) and Milne (2011). However, the

Bodhisatta seems to place greater emphasis on the actions of the birds rather than their physical characteristics.

The dream illustrates the potential difficulties that may arise when individuals lacking in virtue obtain positions of authority. This can result in a lack of ethical governance and moral direction, which can marginalize virtuous individuals under the leadership of those with negative attributes. The analysis underscores the importance of developing virtuous qualities and ethical leadership to promote a more empathetic and equitable society.

In a dream scenario, one may envision a crow enveloped by golden ducks, which are symbolic of protection in some cultures. From a psychological standpoint, this imagery could possibly point to an individual's feelings of loneliness and vulnerability, even in the midst of symbols of good fortune and safety.

Sixteenth Dream: Goats Grazing on Cheetahs

In the sixteenth dream, King Pasenadi dreams of goats grazing on cheetahs, with the cheetahs fleeing in terror at the sight of the goats. This unusual dream reverses the natural order, where the typically weaker prey (goats) triumph over powerful predators (cheetahs). Bodhisatta interprets this as a symbol of the decline of noble leaders, who face persecution and eventual withdrawal from their roles, highlighting the impermanence of power and influence, even among virtuous individuals (Ja 77).

The dream's animal symbolism suggests a shift in the natural order, indicating a significant change. Experts would likely focus on the role reversal's importance rather than individual animal representation (Milne, 2011; Hall, 1953).

From a Buddhist perspective, this dream represents the dangers of corrupt leadership and the shifting dynamics of power. The goats overcoming the cheetahs symbolize the vulnerable triumphing over those who misuse their strength, reflecting the importance of ethical governance. The dream emphasizes the need to protect the innocent and uphold justice, aligning with Buddhist teachings that stress fairness, compassion, and protection of the vulnerable in society.

From a psychoanalytic viewpoint, this dream may reflect the dreamer's fears and insecurities. The goats symbolize a subconscious longing for security and control, while the fleeing cheetahs represent internal fears or threats. The reversal of roles, where the weak overcome the strong, suggests the dreamer's desire to gain control over challenges and adversities in life, highlighting a subconscious coping mechanism for dealing with real-world stress and fear.

Dreams in Other Jataka Stories

It is worth noting that several jataka tales, aside from the Mahasupina-jataka (Ja 77), also underscore the significance of dreams. In this regard, the ensuing paragraphs will expound on the narratives and sections that relate to dreams.

According to the Mora-jataka (Ja 159), Queen Khema dreams of a golden peacock preaching a sermon. So intense was her yearning to hear the sermon that she ordered the peacock to be captured, hoping to make her dream come true. Sadly, the peacock was captured long after the Queen's passing, and she never had the chance to hear the sermon that had stirred her mind in her dreams.

In contrast to the Mahasupina-jataka, the Queen in this tale is driven by her desire to fulfill her dream rather than being afraid of it. She takes proactive measures to increase the likelihood of its realization, hoping it will serve as a prophetic vision. The story does not provide any information on whether the Queen experienced the same dream again over the next seven years. Nonetheless, the dream leaves a lasting impression on her, fueling her quest until her passing. Research suggests that our ability to remember dreams decreases as we age (Waterman, 1991).

The Ruru-jataka (Ja 482), similar to the Mora-jataka, tells the story of a dream but with a unique twist. Queen Khema dreams of a golden deer preaching, and becomes desperate to hear it in real life, even to the point of threatening to die if they cannot find it. The golden deer represents Bodhisatta in one of his past lives, and unlike in the Mora-jataka, he reveals himself to a merchant's son who was saved from suicide. The Bodhisatta convinces the boy to keep the encounter a secret, but when the Queen offers a reward for finding the golden deer, the boy cannot resist. He reveals the location to the King, and the Queen is able to hear the deer preach in real life.

Once again, similar to the Mora-jataka and Ruru-jataka stories, the Mahamora-jataka (Ja 491) depicts the Bodhisatta as a golden peacock living in the woods under the protection of a morning and evening spell. Queen Khema dreams of the golden peacock preaching to her, and she wakes up longing to hear it in real life. Unlike the previous two stories, however, she believes that the King will not take seriously her request if he knows that she saw the golden peacock in a dream. In contrast to the previous two stories, in which the King did not seem concerned about the dream driven by longing, the present story illustrates the King's concern. The only indication that the King is skeptical in the other two stories (and this one as well) is that he asks the Brahmins to verify the existence of such golden animals before he begins searching. Therefore, it is interesting that the Queen chooses to lie about her dream in this story. This is one of the few descriptions of the possibility that someone will not believe her dream. This is an intriguing subject because the truthfulness of dreams is heavily influenced by culture and the authority of the dreamer (Harris, 2003). Her strategy did not even succeed because the Queen died before her dreams came true, just as in the Mora-jataka.

The Rohanta-Miga-jataka (Ja 501) is another story that portrays the Bodhisatta as a stunning golden deer that resides in the Himalayas. This tale also introduces the Bodhisatta's younger brother, who is also a golden deer, setting it apart from the previous stories. As with the other stories, this one recounts Queen Khema's dream of a golden deer preaching to her, leaving her yearning to hear it in person. Additionally, Bodhisatta's voice is described as sweet and alluring, as seen in the Ruru-jataka. Unlike the Ruru-jataka, however, the Queen hesitates to share her dream of the golden deer with the King.

In the Mahahamsa-jataka (Ja 534), there is a similar tale where ninety thousand geese worship the Bodhisatta and reside on Mount Cittakuta. Queen Khema had a dream in which numerous golden-colored geese were preaching the law in a melodious voice. The Queen is excited to hear the preaching but is also worried that asking for golden geese might make her seem insane. Like the previous stories, she pretends to have a craving for a golden goose and claims that she will be unwell until she receives it. She even goes as far as to suggest that she will perish if she does not receive the golden goose and hear it preach. Though not much else ties to the fact that this vision was a dream, it is worth noting that the Queen would use pregnancy as an excuse, considering that dreams can alter dramatically for pregnant women (Maybruck, 1986, as cited in Dagan et al., 2001).

In the Kunala-jataka (Ja 536), Bodhisatta's previous life is recounted as that of a magical bird named Kunala. Hundreds of female birds protected and adored him, but he was cruel and disrespectful towards them. The story highlights the dangers of women through several instances of women he had encountered in his past lives.

In this story, Kunala tells a story about a king named Baka. Within the kingdom Baka governed, there lived a deformed woman named Pancapapa. Despite her deformities, Pancapapa's touch was alluringly soft, and anyone who touched her was overcome with lust. King Baka was no exception. They married, and he began leading a double life - reigning as King during the day and fulfilling his duties as a husband at night by visiting her in the village.

One day, he realizes that he cannot maintain his dual existence any longer. Therefore, he develops a plan to allow the girl to live with him in the palace without jeopardizing his standing with the court for marrying an unattractive woman. He places a beautiful jeweled diadem in the girl's home and dispatches a search team to locate the diadem that he claims was "stolen." When they locate it at the girl's house, they are accused of theft and brought back to the kingdom. When she explains that her husband gave her the gift, she also mentions that she can recognize him only by touch. Subsequently, the King establishes a system where she can touch each male citizen's hand to find her husband. This way, the people are made aware of her special touch and do not pass judgment or disown the King when they learn that he is actually her husband.

It is worth noting the following details: Pancapapa had a dream in which she saw herself as the chief Queen of two kings. After being accepted as the Queen and living in the palace, she did not hesitate to share her dream with the King, just as Queen Khema had done in similar stories. The King then called upon dream interpreters to determine the significance of the dream. However, unbeknownst to him, these interpreters had received bribes from jealous women in the village who disapproved of Pancapapa. They falsely informed the King that Pancapapa posed a threat to him and would cause his death. As a result, the King sent Pancapapa away in a boat. Fortunately, she eventually met and fell in love with King Pavariya from a neighboring kingdom, who made her his chief Queen. The story demonstrates the self-fulfilling prophecy in psychology (Merton, 1948), which suggests that individuals have the power to create their own reality. In other words, because both the King and Pancapapa believed the dream to be true, they made it a reality by acting on it.

The Bhuridatta-jataka (Ja 543) bears some resemblance to the Kunala-jataka (Ja 536) in that it contains little analysis of dreams. Like the other tales in this section, this one features a nightmare that fills the dreamer with dread. In this story, Bodhisatta is reborn as Bhuridatta, the son of the King and Queen of the Nagas. One day, a hunter discovers

Bhuridatta and alerts a snake charmer to his presence. The snake charmer captures and mistreats Bhuridatta. Although Bhuridatta knows he is in peril, he accepts the snake charmer's demands without anger so as to maintain his principles and practices. The snake charmer makes Bhuridatta perform numerous feats, such as changing color and shape and becoming invisible. The snake charmer and Bhuridatta perform for the villagers, earning a great deal of money because Bhuridatta's tricks are astounding. The snake charmer, seeing Bhuridatta's potential, becomes greedy and desires to take him to a large city for more performances.

The Queen is troubled by a vivid dream where a man with red eyes cuts off her arm with a sword and flees with it, leaving a trail of blood. Upon waking, she fears the dream is a warning that something terrible will befall one of her children, particularly Bhuridatta, who she believes is in danger due to living outside of Naga territory. Her concern grows when Bhuridatta fails to return home for several nights.

It has been a month since Bhuridatta left, and his absence is weighing heavily on his eldest son, Sudassana. He notices her despondency and asks what is troubling her. She recounts a dream she had a month ago in which she sensed that Bhuridatta was in danger. It is interesting to note that, as Halliday (1987) writes, dreams can often cause more discomfort when we are awake than during the dream itself. Despite this, Bhuridatta remembers the key details of the dream, such as a man cutting off her arm and running away with it. However, she now interprets the loss of her arm as the loss of Bhuridatta himself, as she could not hold onto "his" hand.

Dream: Unconscious Thought, Desires, and Conflicts

In the Bhuridatta-jataka, like in the Vidurapandita-jataka (Ja 545), dream analysis plays a role. However, unlike the former, the latter offers a more detailed interpretation of the dream. In this story, the Bodhisatta consults with four kings in his past life. One of the kings, King Dhananjaya, has a dream during the consultation. He sees a great tree at the entrance to his palace, with the trunk symbolizing wisdom, its branches signifying virtues, and its fruits representing the five sacred products of the cow. He observes a sea of folded hands worshipping the tree and then sees a man wearing earrings made of red flowers and red clothes. Despite the folded hands' protests, the man approaches the tree with his weapons, cuts it down by the roots, and drags it away. However, in a surprising twist, he later returns the tree to its original location, replants it, and leaves the area.

Some of the dream's meaning is implied in its description - for instance, the trunk symbolizes wisdom, and the branches represent virtues. However, the King himself begins to interpret the dream as a whole. Having spent time in the Naga realm, he sees it as a sign that the Bodhisatta will return that day. He identifies the tree as the Bodhisatta, as no one is wiser than he, and the trunk represents wisdom. The King interprets the man's act of cutting down and replanting the tree as a metaphor for the Bodhisatta leaving and returning to the kingdom. He then orders the entire city to be adorned with jewels and all citizens to welcome the Bodhisatta back. Upon his return, the Bodhisatta shares his adventures with the townspeople.

After the Bodhisatta had finished his tales, the King was eager to share his own dream that had prompted him to prepare for Bodhisatta's return. He recounted the dream to the townspeople, describing a magnificent tree at the kingdom's gates with a trunk of wisdom and branches of virtue. Despite its beauty, the tree had been chopped down by a man but was later restored. The King used this story to preach to the people, urging them to free all those held captive in his kingdom just as the tree had been freed. While it is unclear if these orders are simply metaphors paying homage to Bodhisatta's teachings, the King's dream clearly serves as a guide for governing the kingdom and predicting the arrival of the Bodhisatta.

The Maha-ummagga-jataka (Ja 546) provides a compelling example of a dream that induces intense fear in the dreamer. King Vedeha has a terrifying dream on the night that the Bodhisatta is conceived in his mother's womb, who was the wife of a wealthy man in one of her past lives. The dream features a massive flame at the center that illuminates the entire world, revealing even the smallest objects. During his vision, Vedeha observes the world of mortal men intermingling with the world of gods who worship the flame. These celestial beings exist within the flames without experiencing any burns or pain. The dream shook the King to his core, and he woke up in a state of terror and disorientation.

The King's four sages ask him about his slumber in the morning, and he tells them about his terrifying dream. Among the sages, Pandit Senaka assures the King that the dream represents good news and a sign of future success. The King asked Senaka to elaborate, and Senaka explained that the giant flame symbolizes the wisdom of a fifth sage yet to be born, whose wisdom will exceed all four. Further, he explains that this upcoming fifth sage will be so grand that both men and gods will treasure him.

Dream: Unconscious Thought, Desires, and Conflicts

After a while, in East Town, the wife of a wealthy man named Sirivaddhaka gives birth to a golden child, the Bodhisatta. While viewing this world, Sakka gave the infant Bodhisatta a medicinal herb to inform people of the significance of his birth. Everyone in town was overjoyed to find that the herb could cure all their ailments. Sirivaddhaka considered it appropriate to name the Bodhisatta after this plant, so he named him Osadha Kumara. A thousand other children were born simultaneously so that the Bodhisatta would never be alone. The Bodhisatta grew up playing with these other children, and these children waited on him every day. His beauty was comparable to a statue made of gold by the time he was seven years old. He then ordered the townspeople to construct building after building until finally, a proper city was erected, including an excellent hall for play, a court of justice, a religious hall, and a beautiful water tank adorned with various varieties of lotus flowers. The area appeared as a heavenly garden as he planted trees there. Seven years later, King Vedeha remembered his dream about the four fire columns and the interpretation that Senaka had given him. He became curious about the fifth sage and dispatched his councilors to locate him. Upon discovering the stunning park and garden created by the Bodhisatta, the councilors were convinced that they had found the elusive sage. However, Senaka was apprehensive about finding a sage who was more knowledgeable than him and, therefore, dissuaded the King and others from pursuing the Bodhisatta.

The Vessantara-jataka (Ja 547) features an important dream, though it is not necessarily the central focus of the story. Prince Vessantara, also known as the Bodhisatta, was renowned for his tremendous generosity. He gave away a sacred elephant to a neighboring kingdom, which ultimately led to his banishment from his own kingdom. He and his wife, Maddi, and their children lived a peaceful life in the Himalayan region, where the Bodhisatta began living an ascetic lifestyle. In another kingdom, there lived a couple named Jujaka and Amittatapana. Amittatapana was a good wife, but one day, while fetching water, she overheard the other wives speaking ill of her, which left her feeling hurt and embarrassed. She decided she would not go to fetch water anymore and that they should hire a maid or a slave instead. Since they were poor and could not afford a slave, they considered asking the Bodhisatta for one. Jujaka went to Bodhisatta's original kingdom in search of him, but the townspeople were angry with him. They claimed that the Bodhisatta had been banished because of greedy, selfish individuals like Jujaka. Upon realizing that he had little hope of gaining the favor of the townspeople, Jujaka resorted to deception. He falsely claimed that the King had dispatched him to inform the Bodhisatta that he had been pardoned and could return to his realm. The townspeople were overjoyed by his announcement, and they graciously provided him with provisions, guidance, and counsel on how to locate the Bodhisatta. Jujaka eventually finds Bodhisatta's abode and spends the night atop a hill nearby, eagerly anticipating his meeting with him in the morning.

Maddi, the wife of the Bodhisatta, has a nightmare that morning. This is one of the few instances in these stories where the word "nightmare" is used rather than "dream," even though many of the dreams discussed in this chapter would undoubtedly be considered nightmares. In her dream, she sees a man dressed in two yellow robes with red flowers on his ears. This description seems similar to that of the man in the dream depicted in the Maha-ummagga-jataka (Ja 546). In the dream, the man enters Maddi's hut, grabs her by the hair, and drags her out of it. He then throws her body down on the ground, tears out her eyes, cuts off both her arms, opens her chest, and tears out her heart. Afterward, he walks away with her bleeding heart.

Upon awakening from a terrifying dream, she turns to the Bodhisatta for guidance. Though he is aware of the dream's true meaning - that someone will come to take their children - he chooses not to alarm her. Instead, he reassures her that everything will be all right. As the day progresses, she warns her children to be cautious while sleeping. The following morning, Jujaka arrives and requests that Bodhisatta's children be taken back as slaves. The Bodhisatta, having not been able to be charitable for quite some time, readily agrees.

Conclusion

In modern Western literature, dream analysis is not widely considered as an extensively accepted form of psychological thought. While the role of dreams in memory consolidation and emotional regulation is acknowledged, researchers tend to agree that the significance of a dream is subject to the cultural background of the dreamer and the mental state and motivations of the interpreter.

In the jataka stories, particularly in the sixteen dreams of King Pasenadi, symbols in dreams are not given a definitive meaning associated with waking life. Rather, they are often interpreted as prophetic, with more focus on the actions that occur in the dream than on specific symbols. It is important to note that none of the interpretations provided in this chapter are intended to offer insight into the dreamer's unconscious thoughts, desires, or conflicts. In fact, it appears that the global interpretation of the dream takes precedence over any individual aspect of the dreamer's psyche.

Despite significant advancements in dream research, there remain many unresolved mysteries surrounding the nature and function of dreams. However, by examining dreams in the context of their historical significance and analyzing modern attempts to interpret them, we may gain a better understanding of their potential role in our psychological lives.

References

Barrett, D., & McNamara, P. (Eds.). (2007). *The new science of dreaming* (Vol. 1). Praeger.

Blackmore, S., & Troscianko, E. T. (2018). *Consciousness: An introduction*. Routledge.

Bodhi, B. (1994). *The connected discourses of the Buddha: A translation of the Samyutta Nikaya*. Wisdom Publications.

Born, J., & Wilhelm, I. (2012). System consolidation of memory during sleep. *Psychological Research Psychologische Forschung*, 76, 192–203.

Dagan, Y., Lapidot, A., & Eisenstein, M. (2001). Women's dreams reported during first pregnancy. *Psychiatry and Clinical Neurosciences*, 55(1), 13-20.

Doidge, N. R. (2005). Dreams of animals. In S. Akhtar & V. Volkan (Eds.), *Cultural zoo: Animals in the human mind and its sublimations* (pp. 45-91). International Universities Press.

Edgar, I. R. (2002). Invisible elites? Authority and the dream. *Dreaming*, 12, 79–92.

Fosshage, J. L. (1987). New vistas on dream interpretation. In M. Glucksman (Ed.), *Dreams in new perspective: The royal road revisited*. Uman Sciences Press.

Fosshage, J. L. (1997). The organizing functions of dreaming mentation. *Contemporary Psychoanalysis*, 33, 429-458.

Freud, S. (1955). *The interpretation of dreams*. Basic Books.

Girardeau, G., Inema, I., & Buzsáki, G. (2017). Reactivations of emotional memory in the hippocampus–amygdala system during sleep. *Nature Neuroscience*, 20, 1634.

Greenberg, R., & Pearlman, C. (1978). If Freud only knew: A reconsideration of psychoanalytic dream theory. *International Review of Psycho-Analysis*, 5, 71-75.

Hall, C. S. (1953). A cognitive theory of dream symbols. *The Journal of General Psychology*, 48(2), 169-186.

Hall, C. S. (1962). Out of a dream came the faucet. *Psychoanalytic Review*, 49(4), 113-116.

Halliday, G. (1987). Direct psychological therapies for nightmares: A review. *Clinical Psychology Review*, 7, 501-523.

Harris, W. V. (2003). Roman opinions about the truthfulness of dreams. *The Journal of Roman Studies*, 93, 18-34.

Hartmann, E. (1996). Outline for a theory on the nature and functions of dreaming. *Dreaming*, 6, 147-170.

Hartmann, E. (1998). *Dreams and nightmares: The new theory on the origin and meaning of dreams*. Plenum Trade.

John, J. E. (2000). *Activating the food dream image to feed the subtle body: An archetypal perspective of food imagery and the symbolism as viewed through the cycle of life archetype* (Doctoral dissertation). Pacifica Graduate Institute.

Jung, C. G. (1984). *Dream analysis*, Volume I: Seminars (Vol. 1). Princeton University Press.

Kilborne, B. J. (1981). Moroccan dream interpretation and culturally constituted defense mechanisms. *Ethos*, 9(4), 294-312.

Kramer, E. (1987). *The dream experience: A systematic exploration.* Routledge.

Kramer, M., Hlasny, R., Jacobs, G., & Roth, T. (1976). Do dreams have meaning? An empirical inquiry. *American Journal of Psychiatry*, 133, 778-781.

Lewis, J. E. (2008). Dream reports of animal rights activists. *Dreaming*, 18, 181-200.

Marshall, L., & Born, J. (2007). The contribution of sleep to hippocampus-dependent memory consolidation. *Trends in Cognitive Sciences*, 11, 442–450.

Merton, R. K. (1948). The self-fulfilling prophecy. *The Antioch Review*, 8(2), 193-210.

Milne, L. S. (2011). A storm in the head: Animals, dreams, and desire. *Cosmos*, 27, 61-119.

Moffitt, A., Kramer, M., & Hoffmann, R. (Eds.). (1993). *The functions of dreaming.* State University of New York Press.

Nielsen, T., & Lara-Carrasco, J. (2007). Nightmares, dreaming, and emotion regulation: A review. In D. Barrett & P. McNamara (Eds.), *The new science of dreaming* (Vol. 2, pp. 253-284). Praeger.

Nunn, C. (Ed.). (2009). Defining consciousness. Special issue, *Journal of Consciousness Studies*, 16(5).

Picchioni, D., & Hicks, R. A. (2009). Differences in the relationship between nightmares and coping with stress for Asians and Caucasians: A brief report. *Dreaming*, 19, 108-112.

Platek, B. (2008). Instinct as guide: Animals in women's dreams. *Psychological Perspectives*, 51, 108-118.

Roesler, C. (2018). Structural dream analysis: A narrative research method for investigating the meaning of dream series in analytical psychotherapies. *International Journal of Dream Research*, 11(1), 1-9.

Schoch, S. F., Cordi, M. J., Shredl, M., & Rasch, B. (2018). The effect of dream report collection and dream incorporation on memory consolidation. *Journal of Sleep Research*, 28(1), 1-8.

Schredl, M. (2013). Animal dreams in a long dream series. *International Journal of Dream Research*, 6(1), 59-64.

Schredl, M., & Hofmann, F. (2003). Continuity between waking activities and dream activities. *Consciousness and Cognition*, 12, 298–308.

Van de Castle, R. L. (1983). Animal figures in fantasies and dreams. In A. H. Katcher & A. M. Beck (Eds.), *New perspectives on our lives with companion animals* (pp. 148-173). University of Pennsylvania Press.

Van de Castle, R. L. (2012). Animal figures in dreams. In D. Barrett & P. McNamara (Eds.), *Encyclopedia of sleep and dreams: The evolution, function, nature, and mysteries of slumber* (pp. 36-39). Greenwood.

Waterman, D. (1991). Aging and memory for dreams. *Perceptual and Motor Skills*, 73, 355-365.

Wilson, C. P. (1967). Stone as a symbol of teeth. *The Psychoanalytic Quarterly*, 36(3),

CHAPTER TWO

PATHOLOGICAL GRIEF: THE PSYCHOLOGICAL IMPACT OF LOSS IN JATAKA STORIES

Introduction

Grief is a natural emotional response to experiencing a significant loss and encompasses the various coping stages (Middleton et al., 1993). Although commonly associated with the death of a loved one, grief can manifest in response to different types of losses, such as the ending of a relationship, geographical distance, or the symbolic loss of a cherished concept or belief (Gort, 1984).

The DSM-5, a widely used resource for mental health professionals, includes diagnostic criteria for persistent complex bereavement disorder, also known as prolonged grief disorder. This highlights the consensus among clinicians that grief responses can mimic mental disorders. Additionally, research suggests that a "normal" grieving process can be comparable to a psychological injury similar to trauma. As a result, frameworks used to address traumatic stress disorder may also be applicable when addressing pathological grief or what is commonly referred to as "abnormal" grieving.

In this chapter, some Jataka tales are analyzed and delved into with regard to the emotional state of one of the characters. In each of these stories, a character either goes through a grieving process or helps someone else in that situation. The overarching themes explored in these tales include 1) abnormal or pathological responses to grief, 2) various forms of pathological grief, and 3) methods for treating these experiences.

Pathological Responses to Grief

An atypical reaction to grief that's often seen is what is known as "pathological grief." The use of the term "pathological" implies that certain aspects of grief are dysfunctional or disordered, setting it apart from a normal grief response. Some experts believe that grief can be so intense that it may resemble a mental disorder (Shear et al., 2011; Stroebe et al., 2000; Schut et al., 1991), as demonstrated by the inclusion of Persistent Complex Bereavement Disorder in the Diagnostic and Statistical Manual of Mental Disorders (DSM-5) (Sealey et al., 2015).

Although the diagnostic criteria for this disorder remain a topic of debate, individuals experiencing this condition typically exhibit intense yearning and preoccupation with a lost loved one, a profound sense of emptiness and hopelessness, and difficulty creating and maintaining social relationships (American Psychiatric Association, 2013). In the jataka stories, a number of characters display signs of what may be considered an abnormal grief reaction, which could be classified as pathological grief.

Intense Grief Response

Let us examine the Sujata-jataka (Ja 352) in relation to this theme. The story revolves around the Bodhisatta, the son of a landowner named Sujata. Sujata's father was deeply saddened by the loss of his grandfather, and his grief consumed him. He even created a shrine in his garden using his father's cremated bones, which he adorned with flowers and visited frequently. His mourning took over his daily life, and on days when he went to the shrine, he neglected his personal hygiene and business obligations. This illustrates a man who was willing to put his entire life on hold to mourn his father.

The story depicts Sujata's father experiencing a grief response that bears resemblance to pathological grief. Typically, mourning entails a mix of emotions, including irritability, sadness, regret, and a hollow sensation of loss that is frequently agonizing (Gort, 1984). Beyond the overall unease and diminished abilities, customary mourning also manifests as a general state of disorientation and unease, which is evident in Sujata's father's behavior. Clinicians may become concerned when a person who is grieving cannot come to terms with their loss. According to the DSM-5, this inability to accept the loss is a key diagnostic criterion for Persistent Complex Bereavement Disorder (American Psychiatric Association, 2013). Moreover, when the loss of function has a negative impact on all areas of one's life, it becomes a cause for concern (Wakefield, 2017).

The accepted objective of resolving grief is to reach a state of acceptance regarding the loss (Kübler-Ross, 1969). While there is no definitive timeline for when the grieving process becomes atypical, research on individuals who have experienced loss suggests that approximately 81% experience emotional improvement within six to ten weeks (Clayton et al., 1968). It is worth noting that a key diagnostic criterion for Persistent Complex Bereavement Disorder is that the loss must have occurred at least six months prior, which implies that some level of progress should be evident by this stage (APA, 2013).

The exact amount of time that passed before Sujata took action on his father's grief is unknown, but his father's response was concerning to Sujata, much like a modern clinician would find alarming. Seeing his father in such a state of distress was heartbreaking for Sujata, so he resolved to help him overcome his overwhelming sorrow. Later on in the story, Sujata stumbled upon a deceased ox outside of the city. He began to offer the animal grass and water, placing the nourishment in front of it and instructing it to eat and drink. People passing by would stop and stare, curious as to why he was attending to a deceased animal. Eventually, they concluded that Sujata was possibly insane and warned his father of their concerns about his son's mental state.

Upon learning this, the father redirected his attention from his own loss to his son's well-being. In an effort to comprehend Sujata's unpredictable conduct, he approached him and implored him to clarify. Sujata then conveyed his thoughts in multiple verses, which will be reiterated throughout the course of this narrative. He proceeded to explain to his father that no amount of sustenance or hydration could bring a deceased creature back to life. Words are futile when spoken to those who have passed on. Subsequently, he recited the message of life's transience. The father accepted the inevitability of death and expressed gratitude to his son for providing solace during a difficult time.

Afterward, the father proceeds to recite his own verses, which are then echoed by other recently healed and grieving individuals in the narrative. He expresses how his anguish has been assuaged, his vitality has been renewed, and the source of his suffering has been extracted. His heart is now filled with elation and serenity. He proposes that a compassionate heart and astute counsel can aid in the journey towards overcoming grief. In the following theme, we will delve deeper into this and other methods for resolving grievances.

Regarding the experience of grief, the Mattakundali-jataka (Ja 449) shares similarities with the Sujata-jataka. The former recounts the tale of a wealthy Brahmin who loses his teenage son, leading him to be consumed by overwhelming sorrow. The father would frequent the cemetery and neglect his responsibilities, consumed by a profound sense of sadness as he paced around the ashes of his departed child.

Pathological Grief: The Psychological Impact of Loss

In this account, the father undergoes a comparable experience to the father in the Sujata-jataka, but instead of grieving for his father, he is grieving for his son. Once again, the timeline of events leading up to the Bodhisatta's intervention to console the father is unclear. As a result, it is difficult to determine whether the father's extended period of loss of function is indicative of a pathological grief response or if it is the intensity of his grief that worries the Bodhisatta. This differentiation is significant when considering current diagnostic criteria for Persistent Complex Bereavement Disorder, which places significant emphasis on the duration of mourning (APA, 2013). Nevertheless, the story treats the father's grief response as if it were abnormal.

The sorrowful father was unaware that his dear departed son had been reincarnated into the realm of the divine. A godly offspring came to him, taking on the guise of his son, adorned in regal attire, cradling his head and wailing inconsolably. Overwhelmed by love at the sight of his child, the father inquired as to the cause of his distress.

At this critical juncture, the Bodhisatta initiated his strategy. He expressed a desperate need for wheels to construct a chariot, citing his overwhelming sorrow as an excuse for his inability to procure them. He went on to declare that death would be preferable to living without the necessary wheels. The father then inquired if he could help locate the elusive wheels, to which the son replied that they were none other than the moon and the sun. This preposterous request caused the father to snap out of his grief-induced trance and call out the son for his unrealistic demands. He acknowledged that these impossible aspirations were a lost cause and that it would be better to die than continue down this futile path. It was at this moment that the Brahmin finally grasped the message, recognizing that hoping for the revival of a deceased loved one was as irrational as pursuing the unattainable sun and moon. Once comforted, he became more virtuous and eventually ascended to the realm of the gods after his passing. This method of consoling grief is further explored in section 3.

In the Ghata-jataka (Ja 454), there is a tale of ten brothers who possess an extraordinary strength and ferocity. According to a prophecy, their mother would conceive a son who would bring about the destruction of their country and family lineage. To spare her sons from being killed, the mother claimed that they were someone else's children. This story showcases the cleverness and resourcefulness that can be employed to preserve lives during perilous times. Moreover, it highlights the unwavering devotion and maternal love of a mother who was willing to go to great lengths to safeguard her offspring.

After a long and arduous battle, the ten brothers emerged victorious, and Vasudeva, the eldest, was crowned king of India. However, tragedy struck when his beloved son passed away, leaving Vasudeva overcome with grief. Described as being "half dead," the king was unable to fulfill his royal duties and confined himself to his palace. He spent his days in bed, weeping and mourning for his son, unable to eat or sleep. This intense and prolonged grief is reminiscent of the characters in the Mattakundali-jataka and the Sujata-jataka and may be considered pathological according to modern diagnostic criteria (American Psychiatric Association, 2013). Vasudeva's story illustrates the all-consuming nature of grief and its ability to significantly impact one's life.

In an attempt to snap Vasudeva out of his grief, his brother Ghatapandita devises a plan. He pretends to go insane and roams around the city, shouting for a hare. Upon hearing this, Vasudeva rushes to him and offers to give him any hare he desires. However, Ghatapandita declines, stating that he wants a hare from the moon. Vasudeva refuses to pray for such a hare and would rather die trying. Ghatapandita then explains that mourning and grief over a loved one is as valuable as yearning for a moon hare. He even admits to mourning for something that does not exist. Like many other stories in the chapter, Ghatapandita concludes with a stanza of grief-consolation.

The Loss of a Companion Animal

A similar, but sufficiently different, story to those already discussed is the Migapotaka-jataka (Ja 372). The story revolves around the life of the Bodhisatta as Sakka. During this time, a man lived in the Himalayan region and led an ascetic life. One day, he discovered an abandoned deer in the forest. The man took the deer home and cared for it. He fed, cherished, and cared for it as if it was his own child. After some time, the deer died of indigestion, and the ascetic man was completely crushed. He expressed his sorrow after losing his deer and expressed that he had lost his child.

When Sakka spotted the man, he went to him and told him that sorrow for the dead was not helpful. The ascetic responded that despite the fact that his tears had no immediate purpose, he nevertheless found relief in them. He essentially tells Sakka that the tears make him feel better. He believes that by crying, he is able to release his inner emotions. As a response, Sakka states that tears would not alleviate the pain. The man then realizes Sakka's words and recites the same stanza at the end of the Sujata-jataka. He says that he has experienced a great deal of relief from pain and that his life has been filled with joy and peace.

Unlike the Sujata-jataka, the man in this story acknowledges the relief that can be found in emotional expression, specifically grief. He realizes that it is important to confront his grief and allow himself to express it, rather than repressing it, so that he can heal and move on. Parkes (1965) proposed that one type of pathological grief consists of an inability to express emotional grief completely, which will be discussed below. At the end of the story, the Bodhisatta (in the form of Sakka) reminds him that clinging to sorrow and suffering will not bring him peace or relief but that it is only through acceptance, understanding, and letting go of the suffering that one can find peace.

The Somadatta-jataka (Ja 410) is another story on the theme of abnormal grief responses. The Bodhisatta appears in the form of Sakka, and the main character lives in the Himalayas as an ascetic. He found a young elephant calf one day and brought it home with him. He raised and cared for the elephant as if it were his own child. He named it Somadatta. Over time, the elephant grew to be a large, strong animal. One day, however, the elephant became ill as a result of overeating. When the ascetic goes out to find him a cure, the elephant dies. He returns home to discover that his elephant has died and weeps and laments.

Sakka observes this and wonders at the irony of a man leaving his wife and child to live a life of religious asceticism and yet lamenting the loss of his young elephant. At this point, Sakka expresses his puzzlement as to why the man would live a life of asceticism, free of worldly attachments, and yet still express such an overwhelming grief response toward the loss of Somadatta. It is consistent with research findings regarding the impact of individual differences on a person's vulnerability to pathological grief. Particularly, people with low levels of social support and those who are emotionally dependent on others are more likely to experience pathological grief (Ott, 2003; Fenichel, 1945). This suggests that having a strong social support network and a sense of self-sufficiency can help to reduce the risk of excessive grief. For instance, the presence of robust familial relationships and an expansive social network has been correlated with a reduction in the propensity for pathological grief symptoms to manifest. This man's grief may or may not qualify as "pathological" since his relationship with Somadatta was very much valued. His intense grief may be a sign of his deep emotional attachment to the young elephant calf and his inability to cope with his loss. The deep emotional attachment that the man had with the elephant calf was evident from his intense grief. However, it is clear that he was more vulnerable to such a reaction given his young elephant calf on Somadatta.

He appears to the man and delivers the same message he delivered to the man who lost his deer in the Migapotaka-jataka (Ja 372). He reminds him that grief is not useful. Similar to the man in the Migapotaka-jataka, who mourned the loss of his deer, the ascetic reveals that he finds comfort in his tears. Similarly to both the Migapotaka-jataka and the Sujata-jataka stories, the grieving character is consoled at the end of the story. The man is now full of joy and peace.

Types of Pathological Grief

A second theme that many of these stories share is that pathological grief can take different forms. The following are some types of pathological grief that have been proposed:

Chronic grief is an ongoing and intense form of mourning that can last for months or even years after a loved one's death. It can be characterized by recurrent and intrusive thoughts and memories of the deceased, sadness, and an inability to return to life as it was before the loss. It can exert a substantial influence on both the physical and psychological well-being of an individual. Grief responses that are considered to be "normal" usually include a desire for a resolution. It often manifests in the grieving person feeling hopeful about the future or being able to begin new relationships. People who do not reach this point of resolution after a prolonged period (approximately six months after the loss) are considered to be suffering from chronic grief (Gort, 1984). People who suffer from chronic grief may have difficulty moving on and may experience depression, anxiety, and sleep problems. There are also intense feelings of sadness, guilt, and self-blame associated with chronic grief.

Inhibited grief is a form of grief that is not openly expressed. This type of grief is a form of psychological defense in which a person consciously or unconsciously avoids expressing their feelings of sadness and grief. It is a way of avoiding the pain and vulnerability associated with the grieving process. This pathological grief occurs when there is either no grief response at all or a very small response (Parkes, 1965). Usually, this response is viewed as a defense against the trauma of loss. It is frequently distinguished by the phenomena of numbing, avoidance, and the suppression of cognitions and emotions associated with the bereavement. This grief can lead to difficulty functioning in daily life and can have long-term psychological and physical effects. Although it can occur in anyone, it is most commonly seen in children and the elderly.

Delayed grief is the experience of grief that is postponed or delayed for whatever reason until sometime after the loss has occurred. A delay in grief is typically described as accompanied by a feeling of "numbness." It can be caused by a variety of things, such as a lack of time for processing the emotion because of busyness, a denial of the loss, or a feeling of shock. According to research, delayed grief can manifest in a variety of ways, some of which are delayed by over a decade (Lehrman, 1956; Lindermann, 1944). Delayed grief can have long-term impacts on a person's mental health, leading to increased feelings of sadness, depression, and anxiety. It may also result in experiences of guilt and uncertainty regarding effective coping strategies for managing the loss.

Atypical grief refers to a form of bereavement that diverges from the conventional stages of the grieving process. Although all of the above responses could theoretically be categorized as "pathological" grief, atypical grief responses are characterized by the presence of positive emotions (Gort, 1984). Symptoms of atypical grief may include difficulty expressing emotions, difficulty accepting the loss, feeling numb, avoidance of reminders of the deceased, and a sense of disbelief or denial. In particular, people may respond to grief through overactivity, manic emotional displays, and denial of the loss.

Although not all the characters in the following stories are representative of each of these types of pathological grief, we will discuss some reactions to grief in relation to them.

Chronic Grief

The Mora-jataka (Ja 159) contains an example of a character who is suffering from chronic grief. The story revolves around the time when the Bodhisatta lived in the Dandaka forest as a golden peacock. One of the wives of the king dreams of a golden peacock preaching. She told the king about it the following day, saying that she wanted to hear it in person. The king, who first needed confirmation that such birds existed, sent a hunter to capture this bird. Although the hunter tried his best to capture the peacock, he was unable to do so. This is because the Bodhisatta would recite two protection spells every sunrise and every sunset on a hilltop. Among these spells, one was worshipping the sun, and the other was honoring past Buddhas. Due to these protection spells, when the hunter set snares around the forest, and the Bodhisatta stepped into one, the snare would not close. The hunter was not able to capture the Bodhisatta for another seven years. Once the queen realized that she would never be able to hear the peacock preach in person, she died of grief.

One intriguing element of this tale is the queen's mourning over something she never possessed. In the realm of grief literature, this is referred to as a "symbolic" loss (Gort, 1984). The queen's sorrow revolves around what might have been, and the fact that she never realized her aspirations and desires adds an additional layer of complexity to her grief. Though often overlooked, this form of grief can be just as intense as the grief triggered by the loss of something concrete. Although these types of losses differ from physical ones, the emotional response to grief can be quite similar. For instance, the demise of a beloved pet can evoke the same emotions of sadness, guilt, and despair as the passing of a cherished family member.

Regarding personal differences, it is possible that the queen is accustomed to getting what she wants. Consequently, the situation in which she is unable to obtain what she desires can be particularly upsetting and distressing for her. Studies have shown that individuals who are heavily reliant on others are more susceptible to experiencing unhealthy forms of grief as opposed to those who are socially well-adjusted (Ott, 2003; Fenichel, 1945). Moreover, this thing she is pursuing may be something she has been yearning for more than anything else, and the fact that she cannot acquire it may only intensify her longing for it. It is possible that she has become attached to the idea of having it and may struggle to let go of this idea, even if it is unfeasible. As a result, she may become more resolute in her efforts to make her dream a reality.

The story does not provide clear evidence that the queen passed away due to her grief. It is plausible that her ongoing emotional distress gradually weakened her immune system and stress response over seven years, ultimately leading to her demise. Studies have indicated that prolonged grief disorder, formerly referred to as Persistent Complex Bereavement Disorder, can have negative impacts on overall health (Prigerson et al., 2009). This disorder involves experiencing a prolonged and intense grief reaction that persists beyond a year.

An additional tale that shares striking similarities is the Maha-Mora-jataka (Ja 491), which details the wife's passing from chronic sadness as a result of her unfulfilled desire to hear the golden peacock. This parable is recognized as one of the earliest written instances of a broken heart, attesting to the notion that a broken heart can manifest as a physical ailment. It highlights the potent influence our emotions wield and how they can affect us on a corporeal level.

The indications of chronic grief can closely resemble those of other psychological conditions, including Major Depressive Disorder, Post-Traumatic Stress Disorder, and Separation Anxiety Disorder. To receive a diagnosis of Persistent Complex Bereavement Disorder, it is necessary for the symptoms to be explicitly connected to the loss that the individual has undergone. Suppose the symptoms, such as profound sadness and hopelessness, may potentially be ascribed to Major Depressive Disorder or another emotional difficulty that the individual is enduring. In that case, they may not be considered to be experiencing pathological grief, as per the American Psychiatric Association's 2013 guidelines. Consider this scenario: If an individual with a background of Major Depressive Disorder displays indications of severe sadness, hopelessness, and the like, it is improbable that they are undergoing pathological grief. Such stories portray a range of emotional reactions and circumstances that could have provoked the persistent grief of these characters, but the precise trigger is challenging to ascertain. This ambiguity underscores the intricacy of grief and the challenge of pinpointing a sole origin. Grief is a personal journey that can stem from various events, emotions, and incidents, making it arduous to identify the underlying cause.

It is plausible that, in both narratives, the sorrowful protagonist experiences a recurring pattern of fluctuating between optimistic moments and overwhelming disappointment, ultimately reaching a breaking point after seven years. Furthermore, the prolonged stress of grieving may have rendered the queen more emotionally vulnerable and receptive, according to Prigerson et al. (2009). The prolonged period of mourning could have also weakened her immune system, leaving her susceptible to both physical and emotional afflictions.

Inhibited Grief

While the Sujata-jataka (Ja 352) may be seen as a poignant illustration of overwhelming sorrow, the Matarodana-jataka (Ja 317) offers a compelling exploration of inhibited grief. The tale follows the life of the Bodhisatta within the prosperous household of a merchant. As a young adult, the Bodhisatta experiences the loss of both parents, leaving his brother to oversee the family's affairs. Tragically, the brother, too, eventually falls victim to illness.

In the wake of his passing, his loved ones reacted with great intensity. They came together and mourned with great fervor, their emotions running high and their grief palpable. This reaction is commonly understood as a natural response to loss (Gort, 1984), as the sudden shock of death can stir up profound feelings of sadness and remorse.

In contrast to the others, the Bodhisatta did not display any outward signs of sorrow or distress. Rather, he exhibited an abundance of empathy and comprehension. As a result, his peers began to whisper amongst themselves, questioning the Bodhisatta's lack of emotion and seeming callousness. Because he did not conform to the customary or expected expressions of grief, some assumed that he had no emotional attachment to his brother and even harbored ulterior motives, such as a desire to claim the family inheritance for himself. It is worth noting that these accusations may stem from the notion that not displaying a conventional grieving process is indicative of a pathological response to grief, as stated by Parkes in 1965. Eventually, the Bodhisatta is confronted by these allegations. In response, he reminds the accusers that all living beings are transitory and that death is an inevitable part of life. The Bodhisatta emphasizes the importance of kindness and compassion, as death can come for anyone at any time. He confronts the men with the reality that they, too, will face death and questions why they are not as affected by this truth as they are by his brother's passing. Furthermore, he suggests that mourning for the living rather than the dead is more appropriate and that it is unproductive to cry over a fate we cannot change. A stanza follows, conveying the message to weep for the living rather than the dead. Ultimately, these words comfort the men, and their sadness dissipates.

This story offers a fascinating exploration into human emotions, particularly in how individuals react to death. What stands out is the contrast between the Bodhisatta's internal emotional state and the external behaviors of the townspeople. Rather than viewing the Bodhisatta's apparent lack of grief as a negative pathology, the story invites us to reflect on the benefits of cultivating a sense of detachment from mortal attachments. Through his words, the Bodhisatta emphasizes the importance of accepting death as a natural part of life and moving forward without being weighed down by attachments that hold us back.

Research indicates that understanding how people grieve loss can be influenced by individual differences. Coping mechanisms and strategies may differ depending on past experiences with loss, relationships with the person lost, amount of support received, and cultural background. These differences can impact how people cope with grief, with individuals who have dependency problems or yearning for attention and emotional support being at greater risk for pathological grief responses compared to those who are more secure in their social relationships (Fenichel, 1945). This aligns with the Bodhisatta's message in many of the Jataka stories that accepting the transience of human relationships can help to alleviate the painful and negative emotions associated with grieving.

Grief Treatment Process

One recurring theme in many of these stories centers around finding solace after experiencing grief. Typically, a loved one intervenes to offer support to the grieving individual. This emphasis on comforting and "healing" the person is understandable if the grief is seen as a pathological condition. It seems that the majority of these stories aim to provide guidance on how to cope with grief rather than avoid it altogether. Grief is viewed as an inevitable part of life that must be handled, not prevented. The stories frequently emphasize that even though grief cannot be avoided, it can still be managed in meaningful ways. The overarching message is that grief can be endured.

Cognitive-Behavioral Therapy

In this analysis, we will explore the ways in which various characters find relief from their grief and draw comparisons to modern methods used to treat Persistent Complex Bereavement Disorder, a form of pathological grief. While there is no one-size-fits-all approach to treating this disorder, studies have indicated that Cognitive-Behavioral Therapy (CBT) holds promise as an effective treatment option (Wittouck et al., 2011). CBT is employed to facilitate patients in identifying and modifying negative cognitive schemas and beliefs that might be exacerbating their symptomatology. Cognitive behavioral therapy is based on two key principles: firstly, that certain thought patterns and behaviors can contribute to psychological issues, and secondly, that individuals can improve their mental health by unlearning these patterns and adopting new coping strategies. Interestingly, many of the lessons shared by the Bodhisatta in the stories discussed in this chapter align with these principles. As such, we will examine how some of the grief resolution techniques used by the characters in these stories compare to the techniques utilized in CBT.

In two stories discussed in the first section of this chapter, Bodhisatta presents a framework for overcoming grief. Throughout the chapter, Bodhisatta, in his various incarnations, uses this framework to comfort grieving characters. The framework is similar to CBT, as it involves changing the way people think about death and then changing the way they feel about it. Specifically, the framework encourages thinking about death in a way that allows for pathological and disruptive grief to occur.

For instance, in the Sujata-jataka (Ja 352), Sujata shows his father that giving water or food to a dead ox in an attempt to bring it back to life is futile. He explains that death is an inevitable part of life and that accepting it is necessary for human growth and maturity. The Mattakundali-jataka (Ja 449) conveys a similar message when the son breaks down in tears after failing to obtain the wheels he desires (which turn out to be the sun and moon). To ease his father's grief, the son demonstrates the silliness of his request and compares it to the silliness of mourning. This allows the father to accept that his loss is normal and that mourning is unnecessary.

Both narratives share a common theme: the Bodhisatta employs practical demonstrations to impart Cognitive Behavioral Therapy-like concepts to the mournful characters. Instead of simply lecturing them to modify their thought patterns, he utilizes scenarios like nourishing a deceased ox and beseeching the sun and moon to illustrate how grieving can alter their perception of their loss. By training their minds to think about death in a less harmful and unproductive manner (avoiding intense sorrow), they can better handle their bereavement. Most of the characters follow Bodhisatta's teachings, which is congruent with research indicating that CBT is highly effective in not only managing prolonged grief disorder but also anxiety and Post-Traumatic Stress Disorder (Hofmann et al., 2012; Cahill et al., 2009). CBT assists people in transforming their pessimistic thinking and behavior patterns, and has been demonstrated to be useful in addressing various other psychological conditions such as panic disorder, social anxiety disorder, and obsessive-compulsive disorder (Cahill et al., 2009).

The Dasaratha-jataka (Ja 461) is a powerful story that delves into the emotional toll of grief. King Dasaratha sends his two sons and daughter to live in the forest for twelve years, believing that he will die at the end of that time, leaving his children to rule. However, after only nine years, the king passes away, consumed with longing for his children. This tale demonstrates that grief is a natural response to loss, not just to death itself (as described in Gort's "symbolic loss"). When Bharata, the younger brother who remained in the kingdom, finds his siblings in the forest, he must deliver the heartbreaking news.

Upon discovering them, Rama-Pandita, the eldest brother, remained stoic and did not exhibit any emotional response. Despite the passing of his father, there was no visible indication of sadness or tears shed. This is a rare instance where the absence of grief is explicitly mentioned and only warrants concern if it is deemed abnormal. In such cases, it is important to delve into the root causes of the lack of grief to determine if treatment is necessary. Through the examination of potential sources of emotional turmoil, we may be able to pinpoint underlying factors that could be hindering the experience of grief. As Rama-Pandita contemplated his siblings, he acknowledged that they may possess varying degrees of insight, making it difficult for them to come to terms with the impending news. Thus, he approached the grieving process with tactful empathy and sensitivity, aiming to comfort his family before delivering the devastating news. To help them manage the news, he brought them to the water's edge and shared the bad news with them. As anticipated, Rama-Pandita's siblings were overwhelmed by grief and were unable to contain their emotions, collapsing into tears. Rama-Pandita's actions are significant, as studies have demonstrated that individuals who receive substantial social support are less likely to experience extreme grief reactions (Ott, 2003). By providing his siblings with a strong support system and a sense of belonging, Rama-Pandita helped them handle their grief.

Bharata was perplexed by the varying reactions of his three siblings and turned to Rama-Pandita for an explanation as to why he was not expressing the same level of sorrow. Rama-Pandita, however, conveyed a timeless message of life's transience, similar to the teachings found in the Jataka stories mentioned in this chapter. As in those stories, the siblings eventually find solace and are able to resume their reign over the kingdom.

Preventative Treatment

In the Uraga-jataka (Ja 354), there is a heartening story about preventative consolation. It takes place in one of the Bodhisatta's past lives, where he lived with his wife, son, daughter, daughter-in-law, and a slave girl. Despite their happiness, the Bodhisatta reminded them to follow moral laws, practice generosity and empathy, and reflect on the fleeting nature of life and the inevitability of death. He encouraged them to live a life free of aggression and to face death with courage and acceptance. As a family, they embraced these teachings.

Out of all the stories, this one stands out as the most direct mention of preventative grief counseling. Unlike modern research that focuses on specific threats of loss, this treatment involves practicing certain thoughts well in advance of any potential difficulties. The Bodhisatta wanted his family to be prepared for anything life might throw their way. Some may argue that these practices resemble preventative CBT techniques more than specific grief treatment methods. However, according to the Sujata-jataka and Matthakundali-jataka stories, the Bodhisatta's goal was to help his family view death in a different way rather than simply react emotionally to a specific event, as traditional CBT-based grief counseling might suggest. Additionally, the Bodhisatta aimed to teach his family to accept and understand death as a natural part of life, which is a different approach from the reactive nature of traditional grief counseling.

Once, while Bodhisatta was plowing the fields with his son, the latter gathered the rubbish and set it on fire. This caused much smoke, which irritated a nearby snake. The snake, in a fit of anger, emerged from its hole and bit the young man, causing his death. The snake then returned to its hole. Upon discovering his son's death, Bodhisatta picked him up, laid him under a tree, and covered him with a cloak. He did not cry or lament but instead continued plowing for the rest of the day, keeping in mind the impermanence of life. This exemplary behavior highlights how consistently thinking about a certain event or concept in a helpful and non-destructive manner can help balance emotional responses. Therapists often use this technique, known as cognitive reappraisal, to help individuals manage their emotions and increase resilience. Reappraisal can help reframe the situation in a more positive light, ultimately reducing the intensity of negative emotional responses.

Furthermore, he requested his neighbor to convey to his wife that there would be a reduced m requirement for food today and to inform their family to bring fresh attire, fragrances, and blooms. Upon receiving this message, the wife comprehended that her son had passed away. Despite clutching perfumes, flowers, and food, she did not shed a tear as she gathered the family and led them to the field. Without any tears shed, they shared a meal and afterward placed the body onto the funeral pyre, offering perfumes and flowers before igniting the pyre. The ceremony was held without any mournful wailing.

As Sakka observed the family carrying out funeral rites with stoic composure, he arrived on the scene. Through a series of inquiries, he was able to ascertain the identity of the deceased and their relationship to the family. Upon discovering that the individual was not an adversary but a cherished son, spouse, sibling, and confidant, he commended the family for their noble reflection on mortality. Subsequently, he bestowed upon them the seven treasures and boundless riches, ensuring that they would never have to toil again. In addition to granting them the seven treasures and immeasurable wealth, he also liberated them from the burden of labor.

One fascinating aspect of this story is the absence of mourning. Unlike many other stories in this chapter, there is no typical framework of a grieving character being consoled. In fact, it seems that no one in this tale experiences any form of sorrow or grief. This may resemble the inhibited or delayed pathological grief described earlier in this chapter. As De Vaul et al. (1979) noted, a failure to mourn properly can lead to chronic health problems. However, it remains unclear whether the characters in this story did not feel any grief or if their cognitive training, coupled with the funeral rituals, allowed them to process the death in a non-pathological or disruptive manner. This raises the possibility that cognitive training could play a vital role in facilitating successful grieving processes, and further research in this area could have significant implications for grief counseling.

Other Grief Themes

Funeral Rites

Within this chapter are numerous anecdotes that explore the various funeral rituals that are commonplace. Regardless of whether the grieving process is typical or pathological, these stories consistently depict funeral rites as the most common response to death. Professionals in the field of grief counseling and therapy often encourage those who are newly grieving to partake in funeral rites as they provide a means to accept the reality of the situation, initiate the healing process, and pay tribute to the individual who has passed. Through participating in these rites, individuals can find closure, express their emotions, and mourn in a healthy manner. While it is unnecessary to discuss funeral rites in every story to avoid repetition, it is essential to acknowledge their prevalence.

Loss of Predictability

According to an early theory of grief (Marris, 1958), humans tend to react with grief when they experience a loss of predictability in their lives. As beings who rely on routine and familiarity to feel safe, our brains work hard to create stable environments for us. When we encounter unexpected or traumatic events, our brains are thrown out of balance and struggle to adapt to the new situation. This is why grieving is considered a natural response to sudden and unexpected changes in our lives. When we lose someone or something that disrupts our daily routines, we not only grieve the loss of that person or thing but also the loss of the predictability we once had (Marris, 1958). As per this theory, we humans rely on continuity to make sense of the world around us, and when that continuity is disturbed, we may experience feelings of grief.

Relief after Death

During the grieving process, it is not uncommon to experience emotions beyond just sadness and sorrow when losing a loved one. In some cases, there may even be a sense of relief, particularly when the person has been ill or suffering prior to passing (Stahl & Schulz, 2018). This is because the survivor no longer has the responsibility of caring for their loved one. However, it is important to recognize that these feelings of relief can also be accompanied by guilt and confusion. It is completely normal to experience a variety of emotions, including relief while mourning the loss of a loved one.

The story of Ananusociya-jataka (Ja 328) recounts the life of Bodhisatta growing up in a Brahmin household. Despite his reluctance to wed and pursue an ascetic lifestyle, his parents were insistent on arranging a marriage for him. Eventually, he acquiesced to their wishes and crafted a golden statue of a woman. When he challenged his parents to locate this mysterious maiden, they were taken aback but ultimately agreed to the proposition.

Psychological Aspects of Jataka Stories

In the kingdom's town, once a revered man named Sammillabhasini was reborn as a young girl. Upon seeing a golden image resembling her, the townspeople speculated it was her likeness and informed the Bodhisatta's parents' emissaries. Though Sammillabhasini had no desire to wed, her parents agreed to exchange the statue for their daughter, and she was sent to become the Bodhisatta's spouse.

The two individuals in this tale were forced into marriage, despite their objections, and lived a chaste and pious existence. Following the passing of the Bodhisatta's parents a few years later, he confides in Sammillabhasini that she may inherit all of the family's assets and property as he seeks a life of asceticism. In response, she assures him that she shares his desire to relinquish their wealth and embark on a new journey to the Himalayas. It is clear that the characters in this story experienced a sense of liberation after the death of their parents despite not directly acknowledging it. Their devotion to their parents had constrained their lives, and it was not until the parents' passing that they were able to live on their own terms.

In due time, they both end up dwelling and relying on charity within the royal premises of the city. Unfortunately, after consuming some spoiled rice, Samillabhasini falls ill and passes away alone on a bench in the city. Her passing was a heart-wrenching moment for the townspeople, as she was known for her beauty and grace. They express their grief through tears, wails, and lamentations. On the other hand, Bodhisatta remains composed when he discovers her and calmly sits by her side while eating. When asked about his relationship with her, they are shocked to learn that she was his wife. It is difficult for them to comprehend how a husband could remain stoic after losing his beloved wife, which aligns with modern research on spousal death (Chan & Chan, 2014). Nonetheless, Bodhisatta's tranquil demeanor showcases his internal fortitude and his ability to remain poised in challenging circumstances. It serves as a remarkable example of the power of resilience and determination.

In many of these tales, the Bodhisatta imparts wisdom that bears a resemblance to cognitive behavioral therapy techniques. He begins by reciting verses that highlight the fleeting nature of life: we are all mortal beings, and every breath brings us closer to our inevitable demise. Regardless of how we choose to live, death is an inescapable part of life. Life is also inherently unstable and unpredictable, and we may experience the loss of loved ones. This echoes the sentiments of Marris's theory (1958) about the loss of predictability. Through his teachings, the Bodhisatta challenges the notion that life is predictable and encourages individuals to let go of this belief.

In the last part of the stanza, the Bodhisatta reminds the people of the town to acknowledge the inevitability of loss. However, this also presents an opportunity and a necessity to cherish those who are still alive. The townspeople then perform the funeral rites for her, and the Bodhisatta returns to the Himalayas.

Conflicts in the Portrayal of Grief in the Jataka Stories

This chapter delves into a comprehensive analysis of the stories in the context of psychological research on grief response, different types of pathological grief, and effective methods to alleviate it. While the majority of the stories adhere to the established framework of coping with and overcoming grief, a few stories deviate from this norm.

In the Candakinnara-jataka (Ja 485), the story of the Bodhisatta's life as a fairy unfolds. He is married to another fairy named Canda, and they reside together on the Mountain of the Moon. One day, the king ventures into the mountain in search of fairies and becomes smitten with Canda upon seeing her. In a fit of jealousy, he kills the Bodhisatta and laments his impending death in a stanza. This tragic event leaves Canda devastated and angry at the king when he reveals himself as the killer. Despite the king's offer to live with him, Canda refuses and mourns the loss of her husband. In her grief, she takes the body to a hilltop and weeps. Sakka, feeling her pain, comes to comfort her and restores life to the Bodhisatta.

In this story, Canda has the unique opportunity to witness her husband's resurrection, which goes against the teachings of the other tales. If any other characters had been presented with such a choice, they likely would have taken it, thereby negating the need for grief treatment. Most of the stories featuring the Bodhisatta emphasize the impossibility of bringing the dead back to life and advocate for acceptance of loss, a common theme in both ancient and modern grief counseling (Chan & Chan, 2014). Although the reasons for this tale's deviation from the norm are beyond the scope of this chapter, it is worth noting that not all stories end with the acceptance of loss.

The Mahakapi-jataka (Ja 516) is a unique story that deviates from the typical structure of other tales. It tells the story of a man who raises oxen in the village of Kasi.

Unfortunately, the man's oxen escape without his notice, leaving him feeling devastated and lost. He wanders aimlessly through the forest, eventually reaching the mountains, where he climbs a tree to eat some fruit. Tragically, he falls into a hellish abyss but is rescued by the Bodhisatta, who appears in the form of a monkey. However, the man betrays the Bodhisatta while he is sleeping, attacking him and cracking his skull with a stone. Despite this, the Bodhisatta provides the man with directions to return home and then disappears. The man is left to live the rest of his life as a leper, enduring a great deal of suffering.

This story contains a metaphorical component that echoes the lessons taught in earlier tales. Throughout the various Jataka stories explored thus far, the characters experience loss or death, leading them to grieve. However, the Bodhisatta, in his various forms, imparts the wisdom of life's impermanence, which ultimately brings healing to the characters.

In our previous stories, we have shown how Bodhisatta's teachings (which we likened to CBT) have helped characters move beyond their metaphorical hells of grief. In this story, that act takes on a more literal interpretation.

Conclusion

Within this chapter, the Jataka stories provide a captivating window into the diverse methods ancient cultures utilized to cope with loss and seek solace during tumultuous times. These narratives impart invaluable knowledge regarding both historical and current approaches to grief and its alleviation.

While the terminology and demographics surrounding grief have evolved since the creation of these tales, the core essence of the grieving process remains consistent. Grief is a natural emotional reaction to loss, yet it can transform into a pathological state if left unchecked for an extended period or with heightened intensity, necessitating expert assistance.

Receiving professional support during times of grief can help one to process their emotions in a safe and normalized manner while also providing strategies for managing and coping with the experience. This type of intervention can also be useful in identifying when grief becomes too intense or is not resolved in a healthy way. One of the most impactful outcomes of this support is the shift in perception towards the loss, which is a key principle of cognitive-behavioral therapy.

The Jataka stories offer a rich source of knowledge on the grief response and the various types of pathological grief, as well as different treatment options available to those experiencing it. By exploring these tales, individuals can gain valuable insights on how to navigate grief and provide comfort to those who are grieving. Ultimately, the Jataka stories present an unparalleled and indispensable asset for individuals aiming to attain a profound comprehension of grief and its management.

References

American Psychiatric Association. (2013). *Diagnostic and statistical manual of mental disorders* (5th ed.). American Psychiatric Publishing.

Bosley, G. M., & Cook, A. S. (1993). Therapeutic aspects of funeral ritual: A thematic analysis. *Journal of Family Psychotherapy*, 4(4), 69–83.

Bowen, M. (1991). Family reaction to death. In F. Walsh & M. McGoldrick (Eds.), Living beyond loss: *Death in the family* (pp. 83-102). Norton.

Cahill, S. P., Rothbaum, B. O., Resick, P. A., & Follette, V. M. (2009). Cognitive-behavioral therapy for adults. In E. B. Foa, T. M. Keane, M. J. Friedman, & J. A. Cohen (Eds.), *Effective treatments for PTSD: Practice guidelines from the International Society for Traumatic Stress Studies* (pp. 139–222). The Guilford Press.

Chan, W. C. H., & Chan, C. L. W. (2011). Acceptance of spousal death: The factor of time in bereaved older adults' search for meaning. *Death Studies*, 35(2), 147–162.

Clayton, P., Desmarais, I., & Winokur, G. (1968). A study of normal bereavement. *American Journal of Psychiatry*, 125(2), 168–178.

DeVaul, R., Zisook, S., & Faschingbauer, T. (1979). Clinical aspects of grief and bereavement. *Primary Care*, 6(2), 391–402.

Fenichel, O. (1945). *The psychoanalytic theory of neurosis*. W. W. Norton & Co Inc.

Gamino, L. A., Easterling, L. W., & Stirman, L. S. (2000). Grief adjustment as influenced by funeral participation and occurrence of adverse funeral events. *Omega*, 41(2), 79–92.

Gort, G. (1984). Pathological grief: Causes, recognition, and treatment. *Canadian Family Physician*, 30(4), 914–924.

Hofmann, S. G., Asnaani, A., Vonk, I. J. J., Sawyer, A. T., & Fang, A. (2012). The efficacy of cognitive behavioral therapy: A review of meta-analyses. *Cognitive Therapy and Research*, 36(5), 427–440.

Kübler-Ross, E. (1969). *On death and dying*. Simon & Schuster.

Lehrman, S. (1956). Reactions to untimely death. *Psychiatry Quarterly*, 30(3), 564–577.

Lindemann, E. (1944). Symptomatology and management of acute grief. *American Journal of Psychiatry*, 101(2), 141–149.

Marris, P. (1958). *Widows and their families*. Routledge & Kegan Paul.

Middleton, W., Raphael, B., Martinek, N., & Misso, V. (1993). Pathological grief reactions. In M. Stroebe, W. Stroebe, & R. O. Hansson (Eds.), *Handbook of bereavement: Theory, research and intervention* (pp. 44–61). Cambridge University Press.

Ott, C. H. (2003). The impact of complicated grief on mental and physical health at various points in the bereavement process. *Death Studies*, 27(3), 249–272.

Parkes, C. (1965). Bereavement and mental illness, part two: A classification of bereavement reactions. *British Journal of Medical Psychology*, 38(1), 13–26.

Prigerson, H. G., Horowitz, M. J., Jacobs, S. C., Parkes, C. M., Aslan, M., Goodkin, K., Raphael, B., & Marwit, S. J. (2009). Prolonged grief disorder: Psychometric validation of criteria proposed for DSM-V and ICD-11. *PLoS Medicine*, 6(8), e100121.

Schut, H., de Keijser, J., van den Bout, J., & Dijkhuis, J. (1991). Post-traumatic stress symptoms in the first years of conjugal bereavement. *Anxiety Research*, 4(3), 225–234.

Shear, K., Frank, E., Houck, P. R., & Reynolds, C. F. III. (2005). Treatment of complicated grief: A randomized controlled trial. *Journal of the American Medical Association*, 293(21), 2601–2608.

Sealey, M., Breen, L., O'Connor, M., & Aoun, S. (2015). A scoping review of bereavement risk assessment measures: Implications for palliative care. *Palliative Medicine*. https://doi.org/10.1177/0269216315576262

Stahl, S., & Schulz, R. (2018). Relief after the death of a loved one. *Innovation in Aging*, 2(Suppl 1), 698–699.

Stroebe, M., van Son, M., Stroebe, W., Kleber, R., Schut, H., & van den Bout, J. (2000). On the classification and diagnosis of pathological grief. *Clinical Psychology Review*, 20(1), 57–75.

Wakefield, J. C. (2013). DSM-5 grief scorecard: Assessment and outcomes of proposals to pathologize grief. *World Psychiatry*, 12(2), 171–173.

Wittouck, C., Van Autreve, S., De Jaegere, E., Portzky, G., & van Heeringen, K. (2011). The prevention and treatment of complicated grief: A meta-analysis. *Clinical Psychology Review*, 31(1), 69–78.

CHAPTER THREE

DESIRE: THE HUMAN DRIVE AND ITS CONSEQUENCES IN JATAKA STORIES

Introduction

One of the fundamental principles of Buddhism involves letting go of all desires. The ability to release one's desires is essential to achieving ultimate happiness, also known as nirvana. Desires are defined as yearnings, cravings, or longings for something that is not currently possessed or for something that must continue to be possessed in the future (Herman, 1979). In Western culture, fulfilling one's desires is often seen as necessary. When one is hungry, they eat. When thirsty, they drink. When feeling romantic, they engage in sexual activity.

However, humans tend to repeatedly seek pleasure, also known as the "hedonic treadmill" (Brickman & Campbell, 1971). In hedonistic philosophy, the fulfillment of desires and pleasure are considered the ultimate goal of human existence. The hedonic treadmill refers to the inclination to continue pursuing the satisfaction of desires, even after experiencing negative life events (Mancini et al., 2011). Buddhist teachings caution against this concept by stating that satisfying desires continuously does not address their underlying causes.

Numerous scholars have highlighted the paradoxical nature of this teaching (Herman, 1979), as the desire to stop desiring is, in itself, a desire. However, the purpose of this chapter is not to delve too deeply into this paradox. Instead, this chapter aims to analyze the moral lessons conveyed in various Jataka stories about desire. As previously mentioned, many of these stories depict characters who suffer the consequences of yielding to their desires.

These Jataka stories cover a broad range of desires, from the basic survival motivations shared by all animals (including humans) according to the fitness-for-survival model developed by evolutionary psychology and biology. These motivations include feeding (i.e., satisfying energy needs to survive), fleeing (i.e., avoiding danger or predators), fighting (i.e., competing for resources or mates), and fornicating (i.e., mating and reproducing) (Garvey et al., 2020). This chapter categorizes the stories according to these four basic motivations and discusses relevant psychological research for each theme. Finally, the chapter concludes with a section on stories that explore desire and some neuropsychological research related to desire.

Feeding

The subsection ahead delves into the fascinating topic of our relationship with food and the lessons we can learn from it. Food is a basic human need, and while it sustains us, overindulgence has been discouraged by many religions. Christianity, for example, lists gluttony - the excessive consumption of food and drink - as one of the "seven deadly sins." These sins were originally identified by Christian ascetic Evagrius Ponticus and are considered the most dangerous vices, as they often lead to other immoral behavior (Frank, 2001). Throughout this chapter, we will explore several stories related to these seven deadly sins.

Desire for Food and Drink

The Valahassa-jataka (Ja196) recounts a tale of a goblin town inhabited primarily by she-goblins who posed a danger to lost or shipwrecked sailors. These cunning creatures assumed the guise of attractive human beings and offered food and drink to lure their unsuspecting victims into their town. The story explores the theme of desire, portraying it as unrighteous not because it is inherently evil but because it is used to manipulate people by exploiting their natural desires. While the desire for sustenance is not inherently immoral when faced with hunger and thirst, the she-goblins' actions are deemed immoral since they exploit human desires for their own gain.

The concept of hierarchical needs extends beyond physical or biological explanations and applies to our desires as well. Desires that are especially strong can be categorized as "needs," while more intense desires may be considered "lusts." The classification of desires can vary depending on the situation. For instance, the desire for food and clothing when one is starving and unclothed could be classified as a "need," whereas wanting more food and clothing even when one is already satisfied and has plenty of clothing may be seen as a "lust" (Herman, 1979).

In the Duta-jataka (Ja 260), there exists a character that personifies the primal urges of lust and hunger. The character emphasizes that humans can be driven to great lengths in order to satisfy their physical needs, and that the temptation to indulge in these needs can affect anyone regardless of their position in society. This is a reflection of how all living beings require sustenance and how humans have assigned moral significance to this basic need. The presence of this character in the Duta-jataka serves as a poignant reminder that even the most powerful individuals can succumb to their desires, and that our cravings can easily overpower our willpower.

The Chavaka-jataka (Ja 309) offers an interesting perspective on desire that is only loosely connected to the story's overarching message. The pregnant queen's intense craving for mangoes is the focus here, though the protagonist's quest for the fruit creates a bit of a diversion. However, it is important to note that pregnancy cravings are a completely normal response to unexpected circumstances, much like feeling hungry when deprived of food. During pregnancy, the body undergoes significant hormonal changes, including an increase in estrogen levels that can trigger intense cravings for high-sugar or high-fat foods. These cravings can feel all-consuming, often taking precedence over other needs or desires at the moment.

The Maha-Sutasoma-jataka (Ja 537) contains a rather extreme depiction of the human desire for food. Several characters in the story become obsessed with the taste of human flesh and continue to crave it despite facing punishment and criticism. This story highlights the incredible power of the mind and how it can be influenced by outside factors. The characters in this tale were so taken by the flavor of human flesh that they persistently sought it out, disregarding the risks associated with indulging in it. A symbolic example in the same story is given through a monster fish that accidentally consumes a fellow fish. The taste captivates it to such an extent that it rejects all other kinds of food. This metaphor illustrates the power of the craving for human flesh, which becomes the sole desire of the characters, even in the face of condemnation and punishment.

The Vikannaka-jataka (Ja 233) offers a metaphor for our relationship with food. In the story, a king is eager to feed a school of fish but waits for them to gather so he can do so more efficiently. Just as he's about to offer them rice, a crocodile appears and devours many of the fish. The king is understandably angry and orders the crocodile to be harpooned when it next appears. The order is carried out, and the wounded crocodile eventually returns home and dies. The moral of the story is simple: the crocodile's greed led to its downfall. This message is reiterated in various forms throughout the jataka tales.

Desire for Sugar

Recent studies suggest that sugar may be more addictive than drugs like cocaine (Ahmed et al., 2013). Our brains react similarly to sugar as they do to mood-enhancing drugs, and since most people encounter sugar more frequently than addictive drugs, it can be a concerning issue. The scientific community is divided on how readily humans develop sugar addictions, with some researchers arguing that the increase in sugar consumption is due to easy accessibility rather than a neurochemical dependency (Westwater et al., 2016).

The Vatamiga-jataka (Ja14) tells the tale of Sanjaya, the king's gardener who brought flowers to the king every day. One day, Sanjaya noticed a wild antelope wandering around the king's garden, but it always ran away whenever it saw him. The king asked Sanjaya to catch the antelope, so he put honey on a patch of grass that the antelope liked to eat. After the antelope tasted the honey, it became obsessed with it and only visited that patch of grass.

Sanjaya started feeding the antelope honeyed grass from his hand and eventually gained its trust. He then led the antelope into the king's chamber by leaving a trail of honey and grass. When the antelope was captured, it became scared for its life, and the king used this as a lesson. The moral of the story is that the antelope's overwhelming desire for sugar puts it in danger.

The Gumbiya-jataka (Ja 366) portrays the desire for sugar in a fascinating light. Bodhisatta, a merchant traveling with his companions, warns them beforehand that the fresh baskets of rice and sweet wild fruits they'll come across have been poisoned by demons. He advises them not to eat anything unless they have his permission. During the journey, they find ripe fruit on the trees, and some men eat it without seeking approval. Sadly, those who ate the whole fruit perished, while those who waited for Bodhisatta's permission threw it away. Only those who ate half of the fruit were given special medicine. The story concludes with a reminder that those who ate the whole fruit died, symbolizing our daily indulgences.

Many people consider fruit nature's candy because of its high natural sugar content. There is an ancient tale in the Kimchanda-jataka (Ja 511) about the king of Benares who lived as an ascetic and gave up all of his desires. One day, while sitting by the river, he saw a ripe mango floating in the water. He cut open the mango and ate a small amount, just enough to sustain himself. For as long as the mango lasted, he ate little by little every day while covering the rest with leaves. Eventually, the mango was gone, and he fasted for six consecutive days, which made him very weak. The river goddess took pity on him and allowed him to consume as many mangoes as he desired.

This narrative employs mangoes to specifically illustrate the concept of sugar addiction and how it can be incredibly addictive. Interestingly, this addiction is not necessarily linked to honey or candy but rather to a natural fruit. This has implications for modern Western culture's attitudes towards sugar, as there are moral connotations attached to the type of sugar consumed. For example, eating sugar through naturally sweetened fruits like watermelon and strawberries is seen as more morally superior than consuming sugar through baked goods or cookies (Miller, 1997). This is also evident in the different stigmas that overweight individuals face compared to those suffering from anorexia or bulimia. In Western culture, being unhealthy due to eating less is more morally acceptable than being unhealthy due to overeating (Miller, 1997).

In the Maha-Sutasoma-jataka (Ja 537), the dangers of sugar addiction are depicted through the story of a boy who becomes addicted to the taste of fruit. Upon accepting a small piece of fruit from some ascetics, the boy becomes intoxicated by the flavor and begs for more. To give him a treat before they leave, the ascetics send him a basket containing various fruits mixed with powdered sugar. After consuming these treats, the boy becomes addicted and refuses to eat anything else, eventually leading to his death after going a week without eating. This story serves as a warning about the dangers of addiction and overwhelming desires, not only in terms of sugar but in all aspects of life.

Fleeing

In this section, you may come across some imaginative and unconventional interpretations as the urge for safety, which underlies the fleeing motivation, is a prevalent theme in most of these stories. As a result, fleeing is construed as the yearning to evade peril. While some characters in this section do not explicitly flee from danger, they do endeavor to escape from distressing or hazardous emotions.

Assaka-jataka (Ja 207) explores a unique human desire that sets it apart from the other tales in this collection. This story delves into the longing to reunite with loved ones who have passed away. The protagonist's desperate attempt to escape death places it under the Fleeing section. It follows the tale of a king who is devastated by the loss of his beloved wife, Ubbari. His grief is all-consuming, and he yearns to have her by his side once more. Although the story does not explicitly state it, this intense longing to be reunited with a departed loved one is a feeling that countless people have experienced. The Bodhisatta recognizes this and decides to show the king that his queen has been reborn. The king is overjoyed at the possibility of being reunited with his queen.

The Bodhisatta escorts the king to a tranquil park and enlightens him about the queen's fate. Due to her excessive focus on her physical appearance in her previous life, she failed to carry out enough virtuous deeds and, as a result, was reborn as a lowly dung worm. To convince the king, the Bodhisatta coaxes the queen to speak and recount her past life. Despite having only a faint recollection of her former existence, the queen emphasizes that she has no desire to reminisce about her human life and has no interest in the king currently.

This tale subtly explores the complexities of desire, highlighting their subjectivity. It reminds us that what holds value for one may not for another, as the adage "one man's trash is another man's treasure" is exemplified. Despite being reincarnated as a dung worm, which could be perceived as punishment for past misdeeds, the queen appears content and fulfilled in her new form. As a non-human, she is free from the worries and desires that plague humans. This serves as a poignant reminder that our desires in life are transient and cannot be carried into the afterlife.

Studies have shown that many people tend to overestimate their own abilities when compared to others. For example, most people believe that they are better drivers than average, which is statistically impossible since some individuals must fall below the average (Alicke & Govorun, 2005). When we evaluate ourselves in comparison to others, we tend to make assessments about our skills, circumstances, and overall well-being (Goetz et al., 2014). The use of a dung worm in this story may be intended to underscore the relative difference in our perceptions of our own lives versus those of others. Dung worms are portrayed as inherently inferior to humans in this story. By engaging in this psychological exercise, it becomes clear that fulfilling human desires may not be the key to everlasting happiness.

Within the Maccha-jataka (Ja 216), there is a brief tale where fishermen capture a sizable fish and opt to cook it. As they begin to set up the fire, the fish, lying there, begins to express its sorrow. The fish explains that it is not the flames of the fire that trouble it but the notion of being separated from its mate. It implores the fishermen to release it because the pain of being apart from its beloved is greater than the fear of death. Bodhisatta materializes, hearing the fish's cries, and instructs the fishermen to free the fish.

This narrative exemplifies the importance of human bonding and affection. It also highlights the primal instinct to evade danger and predators, as the fish was on the brink of being captured by its pursuers. In the moment of the fish's passing, its mind was consumed with the anguish of losing its cherished companion. This underscores the undeniable significance of love in human existence and how our feeling of security becomes intertwined with those we hold dear.

Fighting

Within these Jataka stories, instances of physical combat can be found. However, as humans have progressed, the concept of "fighting" for survival has expanded beyond punches and bloodshed. The drive to compete for resources and protect oneself remains at the heart of these struggles. Through the stories contained in this subsection, it is clear that the characters are in pursuit of resources, often in the form of power, which they deem essential to their survival.

In contrast to the other jatakas included in this collection, the Ruhaka-jataka (Ja 191) explores the theme of seeking fame and recognition. As humans, we are often driven by the desire to be admired and desired by others, which is deeply ingrained in our nature. While this may not appear to be an instinctual urge to fight, the pursuit of admiration is directly linked to our competitive nature. We tend to perceive our worth as higher when we are highly desirable to others, which can give us access to better resources. However, an excessive need for admiration has also been associated with narcissistic personality disorder (Back et al. 2013).

This is a tale about Ruhaka, a chaplain whom King Bodhisatta gifted a stunning horse. As Ruhaka paraded through town on his horse, the people were awestruck by its beauty and elegance, singing its praises. The chaplain was filled with pride at the admiration he received. Upon returning home, he shared the story with his wife. Although she had a reputation for being dishonest, we won't delve into that here. She suggested that if Ruhaka dressed like the horse, he too would be adored by the town and perhaps even praised by the king.

The chaplain was subject to ridicule and mockery as he made his way through town, prompting the king to question his sanity and publicly shame him. This left the chaplain feeling humiliated and angry with his wife. While the story takes a negative turn towards women, it highlights the topic of the desire for admiration and praise. Interestingly, those with narcissistic personalities tend to have a high need for self-enhancement and self-promotion, as noted by Back et al. (2013) and the APA (2013). In this case, the chaplain's own desire for status led him down a path of delusion, where he believed that even horse adornments were suitable for his own use.

The Bharu-jataka (Ja 213) tells the story of a conflict over a coveted spot beneath a tree. This tale speaks to the universal desire for space, something that has been sought after by people throughout history. Whether competing for a lease or fighting for territory, our predecessors and modern society alike have engaged in this struggle. The Bodhisatta in this story was seeking alms in the city of Bharu when he discovered a banyan tree. He and his group of followers fashioned a simple shelter beneath the tree and settled there. Another ascetic and his group also took shelter under a nearby tree in a similar manner. When the second tree died, that group of ascetics moved to the first tree, where the Bodhisatta and his followers were already living. Upon discovering their spot had been taken, both groups became angry and began fighting. They eventually resorted to bribing the king for sole ownership of the tree, only to realize how far they had strayed from their principles. Despite having given up worldly desires, they found themselves quarreling and using bribes over a tree. In the end, all of them returned to the Himalayas.

This story highlights the various forms that greed and desire can take. In today's society, people often associate these negative qualities with sex, money, and food. However, there are subtler ways in which we can be greedy, as demonstrated by this tale.

Another story, the Garahita-jataka (Ja 219), does not focus on a specific character's desires but instead addresses how humans are prone to succumbing to their desires in general. In this story, the Bodhisatta is reborn as a monkey and lives among humans for many years before returning to the wild. The other monkeys are eager to learn about human ways, but the Bodhisatta warns them that humans are consumed by greed and a desire for wealth rather than living virtuously. The monkeys are not pleased to hear this and flee. Pursuing riches or desiring more money than one already has is not conducive to leading a joyful or morally upright life.

Despite the abundance of cautionary tales surrounding the perils of sexual desire, it is in fact the pursuit of wealth that proves to be the most insidious hindrance to our moral compass. Scholars have long debated the corrupting influence of money, with some asserting that it holds equal sway to power itself (De Vries, 2007). In contemporary society, it remains challenging to untangle these two concepts when considering their impact on our values and priorities.

The Kamanita-jataka (Ja 228) recounts the tale of a king who, driven by his passion for wealth, sex, and greed, ruled unjustly. This story also details the rebirth of Bodhisatta as Sakka, who, upon witnessing the king's unrighteous rule, devised a plan. He appeared before the king in the form of a young man and informed him of three highly prosperous cities that would be easy to conquer. The king, intrigued by the description of the cities' fertile soil, abundant animals, large armies with chariots and horses, and golden ornaments, pledged to follow the young man with some armies the following day. However, after a few days, Sakka, being Bodhisatta, returned to heaven and was not seen again.

Desire: The Human Drive and its Consequences

The king and his army searched for him but to no avail, and the king fell ill from grief. He was deeply saddened by the loss of glory he could have attained through the conquest of those cities. Sakka, having witnessed the king's poor health, offered to cure him. The king explained that his illness stemmed from greed. In response, Bodhisatta warned him about the dangers of desire, stating that only by curing his greed and desire could he be healed. Furthermore, he explained that desire is the "root of all evil," and those who increase their desires are destined for hell. The king was frightened and ruled righteously until his death.

The protagonist in this tale displays an intense yearning for authority that aligns with the psychological concept of the desire to assert influence, impact, or control over others (McClelland, 1985; Sosik & Dinger, 2007). Research has identified two types of charismatic leaders, socialized and personalized, though it's unclear whether the king in this story fits either category (House & Howell, 1992). While we won't delve into the ethics of leadership traits, it's clear that the king resembles a personalized leader who leverages his power to subdue his rivals and gain control over others. The "unjust decisions" mentioned in the tale may stem from the king's hunger for power and control over those around him.

In the Kama-jataka (Ja 467), there is a tale of a young man who was made viceroy but was unhappy with his position. He longed to seize the kingdom and become its ruler. At his brother's request, the king agreed to grant him control over the kingdom. However, his ambition only grew, and he soon desired not just one but two or even three kingdoms. His greed was insatiable, and he ruled unjustly. When Sakka noticed this, he intervened and suggested a plan to the king. He informed the king of three prosperous cities that he could conquer, but disappeared when the caravan was assembled to go in search of them. The young man also became physically ill, and the Bodhisatta advised him that only by curing his greed could he be cured of his physical ailments.

In addition, the Bodhisatta cautions the king that our desires will only multiply as long as we indulge them. His teachings stress the significance of relinquishing desires to achieve happiness. Freedom from the endless cycle of desire fulfillment can lead to a more contented life.

In the Mandhatu-jataka (Ja 258), we see a king named Mandhata who is always discontented. Even after receiving control of the heavenly kingdom from the heavenly kings, he continues to yearn for more power. Eventually, Sakka grants him control over half of the kingdom of the Thirty-three gods, and they rule together for millions of years. However, Mandhata's desire for complete control proves to be too great, and he ultimately fails in his quest to kill Sakka. In the end, Mandhata dies as an old man, unfulfilled and consumed by his unchecked desires.

Fornicating

The stories in this subsection mainly serve as cautionary tales about sexual desires. In recent years, Christian and Jewish faith-based communities have started discussing sexual education as a relevant topic (Haffner, 2011). In many Asian-American communities in the West, sexuality is still considered a taboo topic (Lee, 2006). While Buddhist views on sexuality differ from those of the Abrahamic religions, their stance on desire remains consistent. Sexual desire is viewed as a natural human experience that is often suppressed by societal stigmas and cultural influences (Wilson, 2003).

Aside from religious beliefs, the subject of sexual desire has garnered significant attention in scientific and clinical circles (Kaplan, 1979). The exploration of sexual desire is a crucial aspect of studying all forms of human relationships (Stuart et al., 1987). It remains one of the most complex aspects of modern human nature, as evidenced by its prominent role in numerous jataka tales.

One of the classic parables found in many Jataka stories is the Mudulakkhana-jataka (Ja 66). It tells the story of a Bodhisatta who was reborn into a wealthy Brahmin family. The Bodhisatta gave up all his desires and lived a life of solitude and austerity. When he grew up, he went to the town to buy salt and vinegar and was invited to have dinner with the king. He enjoyed the delicious food so much that he was allowed to stay in the garden for 16 years. One day, the king had to leave for business, and his wife took care of the Bodhisatta in his absence. While preparing dinner for him one night, she decided to bathe and apply perfume since he was running late. When he arrived, she rushed to attend to him, and in the process, her robe fell off, leaving her naked. Similar events are recounted in the Samkappa-jataka (Ja 251) and the Harita-jataka (Ja 431).

Afterward, he became completely consumed with desire for the queen, to the point where he didn't even eat. He lay in the garden for a full week, consumed by an intense lust he had never experienced before. When the king returned and saw the Bodhisatta's state, the Bodhisatta revealed that he was sick due to his longing for the queen. The king then granted the Bodhisatta permission to have her and gave her away. However, he advised the queen to make sure she understood her task and to ensure the holy man was saved.

In due time, they settle into a squalid abode that was bestowed upon them by the king. The woman is exceedingly fastidious, tasking the Bodhisatta with even the most trivial chores to ensure the house is habitable. This eventually takes a toll on him, until she reminds him of his sacred life, and he suddenly reverts to his former insightful state.

Afterward, he escorts the queen back to the king and reveals to him the errors of his ways. Specifically, his all-consuming longing for the queen was the root of his mistake. He came to the realization that when one becomes consumed by desire, virtuous behavior is forgotten, and living a holy life becomes unattainable. In the Samkappa-jataka (Ja 251), the Bodhisatta acknowledges his grave error in succumbing to his own overwhelming desire and retreats to the Himalayas to live a solitary life. In the Harita-jataka (Ja 431), the dangers of lust are emphasized, and the Bodhisatta eventually recovers from his intense desire.

The Cullapalobhana-jataka (Ja 263) recounts the story of an ascetic who, upon encountering a naked woman for the first time, falls prey to desire. However, he later renounces this desire after receiving a warning from the Bodhisatta about the perils of sexual desire. Meanwhile, in the Ummadanti-jataka (Ja 527), men are depicted as being enraptured and overwhelmed by passion upon beholding the stunning and awe-inspiring beauty of Ummadanti.

The Udancani-jataka (Ja106) tells the story of a father and son, where the son desires a woman. Every day, the son would bring fruits and light a fire, but he stopped when the woman approached him and allegedly tried to lure him away. The son sought the Bodhisatta's permission, and the father realized his son was lovesick. He used a strategy similar to that of the king in Mudulakkhana-jataka (Ja 66), allowing the son to accompany the woman but warning him that she would be demanding and he would be expected to complete various tasks for her. When the son found it unbearable, he retreated to the hermitage, and the Bodhisatta praised his wisdom upon his return.

In the Samiddhi-jataka (Ja 167), the Bodhisatta is a Brahmin's son who has dedicated himself to a religious life and developed spiritual abilities while living in the Himalayas. One day, after bathing and drying himself in the sun, a beautiful nymph from the realm of the gods becomes entranced by his perfect appearance and attempts to seduce him. She invites him to indulge in the pleasures of her world, but the Bodhisatta wisely declines, knowing that it is better to pursue enlightenment than to give in to fleeting pleasures. The nymph disappears in response to his steadfastness. This Jataka story serves as a reminder of the importance of resisting temptation on the path to enlightenment.

In the Manicora-jataka (Ja194), the Bodhisatta is living his life as a householder in a village with his beautiful wife, Sujata. In the course of their travels through a city, the king became so enamored with her that he wanted to do anything to get her, including getting rid of her husband. So, he devised a plan and had the king's jeweled crest planted in the wagon of the Bodhisatta and Sujata. When the king caused an uproar in search of his lost (or possibly stolen) crest, they searched the city for it and eventually located it in the wagon of the Bodhisatta. Assuming he was a thief, they arrested him, beat him, and expelled him from the city.

Townspeople called for his beheading as a punishment for this crime. It was an agonizing and demoralizing experience for Sujata as she realized how helpless she was in this situation. She became angry at the unfair treatment she was receiving and cried out to the gods, saying that they had abandoned her.

The story mentioned in the previous message presents an interesting case of desire, which is not necessarily the central theme of the story but rather a symptom of overall unrighteousness. The tale narrates the unrighteous king's malicious plan, driven by his unrelenting desire for Sujata, which ultimately leads to his downfall. However, the Bodhisatta and Sujata's mutual desire for each other is not depicted as immoral or unrighteous, as they lead a joyous and unified life together.

This narrative of marital desire is of significant interest to psychological research, which has long sought to understand the role of sexual desire in long-term romantic relationships. Studies have shown that the presence of sexual desire within the relationship enhances long-term marital satisfaction (Brezsnyak & Whisman, 2010). This implies that marriages lacking sexual desire may be more likely to be unsatisfying. However, it is essential to note that sexual desire is distinct from having sex. In this story, the Bodhisatta's marriage is depicted as happy and joyful, indicating the presence of plenty of sexual desire, regardless of whether it was acted upon or not.

Interestingly, the Manicora-jataka (Ja194) and Culla-Bodhi-jataka (Ja 443) share a similar story, but there is a clear contrast between them. While the former does not mention the Bodhisatta's wife, the latter specifically states that the couple lived happily together without giving in to their desires. Despite this difference, both stories have similar outcomes - the Bodhisatta and his wife enjoy a long and happy life together. The Udaya-jataka (Ja 458) also depicts the Bodhisatta as being married without giving in to temptation. These stories suggest that strong marital desire may have played a role in the Bodhisatta's enduring relationship with his wife (Brezsnyak & Whisman, 2010).

General Desires from all Senses

We have explored the representation of desire in the Jataka stories with regard to the four fundamental motivations. Nevertheless, there exist certain overarching tales that impart valuable lessons on the subject of desire, which do not neatly align with the categories mentioned above. In this section, we shall delve into these narratives whilst also examining some of the cognitive processes associated with desire and contentment.

The Telapatta-jataka (Ja 96) tells a story about indulging all five senses. The protagonist, the Bodhisatta, was uncertain whether he would ever rule as the king's youngest son. The Pacceka Buddhas suggested that he could reign in the city of Takkasila, but only if he survived a treacherous journey. The Pacceka Buddhas warned of a village of ogresses on the way, who lure male travelers with food and drinks and then devour them. These ogresses appeal to the senses, using beautiful sights, sounds, scents, tastes, and soft cushions to entice men. The only way to survive is to control all the senses.

Bodhisatta embarked on a journey with five of his companions, including the ogresses. Unfortunately, one of his companions, who was captivated by physical beauty, was seduced by an ogress and lost his life. Later on, another companion, who had a passion for music, was lured by the beautiful melodies played by the ogresses and met a similar fate. Lastly, one of the companions fell victim to an ogress who carried the most delightful perfumes and fragrances. The alluring scents proved too much for him, and he was consumed by the ogress.

As the group journeyed on, they came across another ogress. A booth of delectable food caught the eye of one companion who had a weakness for gourmet cuisine. Unfortunately, like the previous victim, he, too, fell prey to the trap and was devoured. Eventually, the Bodhisatta and the remaining companion came upon an ogress seated on luxurious velvet cushions. Despite the companion's attempt to comfort her, he, too, met the same tragic fate. The Bodhisatta was the only one left from the original group. The ogresses tried to lure him with the impersonation of his "wife," who even went so far as to bear a child. However, the Bodhisatta remained steadfast and did not succumb to temptation.

Eventually, the ogress manages to lure and slay the king, paving the way for her fellow ogresses to invade the palace and consume everything in sight. It is only then that the crowd realizes the gravity of the situation and the folly of the king's decision to let the ogresses run amok. However, when the Bodhisatta arrives, the people are quick to recognize his journey's success, achieved through control of his senses and desires. As a result, they choose him as the new ruler of Takkasila, a decision which he accepts.

Desire: The Human Drive and its Consequences

Recent studies examining the effects of reward on the human brain have revealed that, while different areas of the brain are linked to each of the five senses, there is a specific region called the orbitofrontal cortex that is responsible for combining sensory input (Kringelbach, 2005). Using this understanding, we can deduce that the brothers in this tale, who have a strong affinity for food, would be particularly susceptible to the ogresses. This is because the desire for food often involves input from multiple senses, such as the aroma, visual appeal, or descriptions in advertising, which can trigger cravings and anticipation.

The Bhadra-Ghata-jataka (Ja 291) highlights the perils of desire in an indirect manner. The story revolves around the Bodhisatta's son, who turned to gambling, gluttony, and an overall immoral lifestyle after his father's demise. He was reborn as Sakka in heaven, but seeing his son in distress, he came to earth and gifted him a Wishing Cup. He promised his son that the cup would fulfill all his desires and make him eternally wealthy. The son cherished the cup and drank from it constantly. However, one day, he threw it in a drunken stupor, shattering it and ruining his life. Though the story does not explicitly mention "desire," it serves as a reminder that even with unlimited access to fulfilling one's desires, true happiness and contentment cannot be achieved. The son's dependence on the cup can represent any addictive substance like food, sex, or drugs. Once that substance is taken away, the person must confront themselves.

The Silavimamsa-jataka (Ja 330) offers a metaphor for the perpetual nature of desires and their inability to provide lasting satisfaction. In the story, the Bodhisatta, an ascetic, observes a hawk snatching a piece of meat from a butcher's shop, which leads to other birds competing for the meat until it is dropped, and the cycle repeats. One bird that lets go of the meat is left in peace while the others continue to fight over it. This tale illustrates the importance of letting go of worldly desires and not allowing them to control our lives in order to maintain inner peace.

The three faces of desire are well-illustrated by a metaphor (Schroeder, 2004). These three faces include pleasure, reward, and motivation, and while the stories in this chapter approach desire differently, the animal metaphor elegantly ties them all together. Motivation is a key component in pursuing a desire and is discussed in this chapter in relation to our four primary motivations: feeding, fleeing, fighting, and fornicating. Thus, motivation is present in every story, such as the birds' desire for food, which satisfies a basic need and motivation.

The following element to consider is pleasure - the feeling of contentment that arises when a want is fulfilled. In the story, the birds' joy is palpable as they finally get their beaks on the coveted piece of meat. The food is likely both delicious and nourishing. (It could be argued that the chickens' pleasure is incomplete, given that they keep dropping the meat. However, for the sake of comparison, let us assume that each time a bird picks up the piece, it is able to consume some of it.) Additionally, reward is the gratification that follows pleasure - the third aspect of desire. While it may be tempting to view the two as interchangeable, they are, in fact, distinct processes.

Studies on the brain's reward system suggest that various stimuli, such as food, sex, and social interaction, can trigger a rewarding response. In this chapter, we have explored the three types of desire and their fundamental nature. When a desire is fulfilled, and satisfaction is experienced, the reward pathways in the brain are activated, increasing the likelihood of seeking out that reward in the future. This process forms the basis of addiction, though not everyone who consumes addictive substances will become addicted. Notably, Buddhist teachings advocating for the release of desires may have neurocognitive advantages in terms of preventing dependence and addiction.

The Sattubhasta-jataka (Ja 402) illustrates the sixteen desires that can never be satisfied in this world. Instead of delving into each of these desires individually, they serve to demonstrate the never-ending cycle of desire fulfillment. The overarching message in this subsection is to break away from this cycle. This theme resonates in the Indriya-jataka (Ja 423), which states: "Who, through desire, obeys the senses' sway, loses both worlds and pines his life away." This phrase encapsulates the essence of all the stories in this paragraph, which state that yielding to the cycle of desire is not conducive to a meaningful and virtuous life. In fact, it can be actively detrimental. The tale concludes with a character reflecting on his life, saying: "O king, through a desire for happiness, I caused misery to others, and I have even become the ghost of a man in this life."

Conclusion

A fundamental principle for leading a fulfilling and meaningful life is to manage and regulate one's desires. This suggestion is not only endorsed by spiritual doctrines but also by scientific findings across multiple domains, including developmental psychology, social psychology, cognitive neuroscience, and neuropsychology.

Various desires can take shape in different ways, ranging from a basic desire for sustenance when one is hungry to more complex desires such as the longing for attention or acknowledgment from others. Yet, regardless of the type of desire, the exploration and fulfillment of these desires activate similar neural pathways in the brain.

Through practicing mindfulness in our pursuit and fulfillment of desires, we can develop a greater sense of self-awareness and attain a more harmonious and satisfying existence. It is important to note that this does not require us to stifle our desires completely but rather to recognize and distinguish between authentic needs and superficial wants. By doing so, we can steer clear of the pitfalls of fleeting pleasures and concentrate on attaining enduring objectives that resonate with our beliefs and ambitions.

References

Ahmed, S. H., Guillem, K., & Vandaele, Y. (2013). Sugar addiction: Pushing the drug-sugar analogy to the limit. *Current Opinion in Clinical Nutrition & Metabolic Care*, 16(4), 434-439.

Alicke, M. D., & Govorun, O. (2005). The better-than-average effect. In M. D. Alicke, D. A. Dunning, & J. I. Krueger (Eds.), *The self in social judgment* (pp. 85–106). New York, NY: Taylor & Francis.

American Psychiatric Association. (2013). *Diagnostic and statistical manual of mental disorders* (5th ed.). Arlington, VA: American Psychiatric Publishing.

Back, M. D., Küfner, A. C., Dufner, M., Gerlach, T. M., Rauthmann, J. F., & Denissen, J. J. (2013). Narcissistic admiration and rivalry: Disentangling the bright and dark sides of narcissism. *Journal of Personality and Social Psychology*, 105(6), 1013-1037.

Brezsnyak, M., & Whisman, M. A. (2004). Sexual desire and relationship functioning: The effects of marital satisfaction and power. *Journal of Sex & Marital Therapy*, 30(3), 199-217.

Brickman, P., & Campbell, D. T. (1971). Hedonic relativism and planning the good society. In M. H. Appley (Ed.), *Adaptation level theory: A symposium* (pp. 287–302). New York, NY: Academic Press.

De Vries, M. K. (2007). Money, money, money. *Organizational Dynamics*, 36(3), 231-243.

Frank, L. (2001). The evolution of the seven deadly sins: From God to the Simpsons. *The Journal of Popular Culture*, 35(1), 95-105.

Garvey, P. M., Banks, P. B., Suraci, J. P., Bodey, T. W., Glen, A. S., Jones, C. J., McArthur, C., Norbury, G. L., Price, C. J., Russell, J. C., & Sih, A. (2020). Leveraging motivations, personality, and sensory cues for vertebrate pest management. *Trends in Ecology & Evolution*, 35(11), 990-1000.

Goetz, T., Ehret, C., Jullien, S., & Hall, N. C. (2006). Is the grass always greener on the other side? Social comparisons of subjective well-being. *The Journal of Positive Psychology*, 1(4), 173–186.

Haffner, D. W. (2011). Dearly beloved: Sexuality education in faith communities. *American Journal of Sexuality Education*, 6(1), 1-6.

Herman, A. L. (1979). A solution to the paradox of desire in Buddhism. *Philosophy East and West*, 29(1), 91-94.

House, R. J., & Howell, J. M. (1992). Personality and charismatic leadership. *The Leadership Quarterly*, 3(1), 81–108.

Kaplan, H. S. (1979). *Disorders of sexual desire*. New York, NY: Brunner/Mazel.

Kringelbach, M. L. (2005). The human orbitofrontal cortex: Linking reward to hedonic experience. *Nature Reviews Neuroscience*, 6(9), 691-702.

Lee, B. (2006). Teaching justice and living peace: Body, sexuality, and religious education in Asian-American communities. *Religious Education*, 101(3), 402-419.

Mancini, A. D., Bonanno, G. A., & Clark, A. E. (2011). *Stepping off the hedonic treadmill. Journal of Individual Differences*, 32(3), 144-153.

McClelland, D. C. (1985). *Human motivation*. Glenview, IL: Scott, Foresman.

Miller, W. I. (1997). Gluttony. *Representations*, 60(1), 92-112.

Nestler, E. J., & Malenka, R. C. (2004). The addicted brain. *Scientific American*, 290(3), 78-85.

Schroeder, T. (2004). *Three faces of desire*. New York, NY: Oxford University Press.

Sosik, J. J., & Dinger, S. L. (2007). Relationships between leadership style and vision content: The moderating role of need for social approval, self-monitoring, and need for social power. *The Leadership Quarterly*, 18(2), 134-153.

Stuart, F. M., Hammond, D. C., & Pett, M. A. (1987). Inhibited sexual desire in women. *Archives of Sexual Behavior*, 16(1), 91–106.

Volkow, N. D., & Morales, M. (2015). The brain on drugs: From reward to addiction. *Cell*, 162(4), 712-725.

Westwater, M. L., Fletcher, P. C., & Ziauddeen, H. (2016). Sugar addiction: The state of the science. *European Journal of Nutrition*, 55(2), 55-69.

Wilson, L. (2003). Buddhist views on gender and desire. In R. J. Davidson & S. R. Grossman (Eds.), *Sexuality and the world's religions* (pp. 133-175). Santa Barbara, CA: ABC-CLIO.

CHAPTER FOUR

PSYCHOLOGICAL DISORDER: MENTAL HEALTH CHALLENGES IN JATAKA STORIES

Introduction

The interdisciplinary field of psychopathology combines insights from various natural and social sciences, including psychology, psychiatry, neuroscience, epidemiology, and sociology. This approach enables researchers better to understand the underlying causes of mental health issues and develop more effective treatments and interventions. It is worth noting that social norms play a role in defining what is considered abnormal psychological behavior, and these norms can change over time due to cultural and social influences, as well as medical advancements. As a result, behaviors that were once considered abnormal may now be seen as normal, and vice versa. For example, what was once seen as abnormal behavior a few decades ago may now be considered normal.

Psychopathology is concerned with identifying patterns of thinking, decision-making, behavior, or experience that deviate from the norm (Schultze-Lutter et al., 2018). It is important to consider an individual's social and cultural norms to determine whether certain behaviors are problematic or require intervention. Mental health professionals use a variety of tools and techniques to assess and diagnose psychopathology and typically treat it with a combination of medication and psychotherapy. Notably, what is considered abnormal in one country may not be in another, and cultural norms can contribute to the development of abnormal patterns of thinking and behavior.

Throughout history, mental illness and disorders of the mind have remained a perplexing subject for scientists, religious leaders, teachers, philosophers, doctors, and other individuals who strive to comprehend the human experience (Farreras, 2022). The complexity of mental illness and its causes, which can stem from biological and genetic factors to psychological factors, make it a challenging issue to diagnose and treat. Moreover, the stigma surrounding mental health often discourages individuals from addressing their mental health concerns or seeking assistance. There has been significant attention given to the understanding of how psychological disorders develop and how they can be effectively treated and cured. This has led to extensive research and investment in the prevention and treatment of mental health issues. Within some of the stories, we will find examples of individuals who have been cured or relieved of their symptoms. This chapter aims to examine the behaviors and experiences of specific characters through the framework of the Diagnostic and Statistical Manual of Mental Disorders (DSM-5; APA, 2013; Lopez et al., 2006).

Understanding the symptoms of various psychological disorders is crucial for scientists and clinicians in order to determine the most effective treatments. Moreover, comprehending the symptoms of a particular disorder can improve the accuracy of future diagnoses by other clinicians. It is important to keep in mind, however, that cultural differences in mental health and the unique ways in which mental health is expressed across different cultures may not always be considered by the DSM. Despite this limitation, Western understandings of these behaviors within the context of the DSM-5 will be applied, even if the contemporary setting differs from the original setting of the stories. It is worth noting that the DSM primarily contains clinical and research findings obtained in the West, primarily the US. In this chapter, we will also explore some of the treatment options available for the discussed disorders.

Attachment Disorder

In the Asatamanta-jataka (Ja 61), we learn of the Bodhisatta's role as a teacher. A young boy was raised with great care within a Brahmin household and completed his education at the age of sixteen. Upon returning to his mother, she sought to impart to him the dangers of women. The mother convinced her son that he had yet to learn the Dolour Texts and urged him to seek out his teacher for further instruction.

Bodhisatta, a renowned teacher, tended to his ailing mother in her old age while they resided in the forest. He diligently bathed her, cooked for her, dressed her, and provided for her every need. Sadly, his kindness caused his neighbors to become resentful, and as a result, they forced him and his mother to seek refuge in the forest.

One day, while in the forest, the student came, and the teacher inquired about the reason for his visit. The student explained that he was there to learn the Dolour Texts. Upon hearing this, the wise teacher recognized that his mother was sending him a message to be wary of women, and he instructed the student to care for his mother henceforth. He also advised the student to praise his mother's beauty daily.

The following account depicts a mother fixated on a student, unconcerned with societal norms, and focused on her own pleasure. The story portrays her in a negative light due to her attempt to seduce the Bodhisatta's disciple. However, there is no indication that her love and desire for the Bodhisatta have caused any psychological disturbances, as discussed in Kunala-jataka (Ja 536). While the woman exhibits behaviors suggestive of attachment issues, there is no explicit mention of any mental or psychological problems affecting any of the characters. The story suggests flaws in character among those involved, but it is unclear whether these shortcomings stem from social or psychological issues. Nevertheless, certain actions displayed by the characters may indicate struggles with attachment.

It is possible that the boy's upbringing did not foster a healthy attachment style in adulthood. Studies have shown that reactive attachment disorder (RAD) can emerge in early and middle childhood due to maltreatment, adoption, poor quality of caregiving, and interactions with adults in early life (Zeenah & Gleason, 2010). Furthermore, RAD can manifest through inhibited or disinhibited interactions with unfamiliar adults. For example, inhibited interactions may appear as extreme shyness or a reluctance to engage in adult social interactions or venture away from the parental home. However, the young boy does not exhibit these characteristics as he leaves home at sixteen to pursue education and embrace an independent ascetic lifestyle. He spends his life traveling and preaching, displaying no signs of inhibited behavior. He is compassionate, loving, and patient with everyone, regardless of status or background.

Reactive attachment disorder is characterized by various signs and symptoms, including disinhibited interactions with adults, limited social and emotional engagement, avoidance of eye contact, resistance to physical affection, and a lack of emotional and physical responsiveness in children as young as infancy (Zeenah & Gleason, 2010). In disinhibited or discriminating social patterns, children may form attachments with unfamiliar adults and exhibit overly familiar behavior or fail to contact their caregivers regularly or at all. In this story, The Bodhisatta's student displays obedience to his mother and independence and gullibility toward strangers. He immediately returns to his teacher to learn about the Dolour Texts but does not question the teacher's motives when instructed on how to behave around the elderly woman.

Antisocial Personality Disorder (Psychopathy)

The Labhagaraha-jataka (Ja 287) is a concise yet impactful tale that carries a profound message. It follows a 16-year-old Bodhisatta who has completed his religious education. One day, a young man approaches him, seeking guidance on how to attain holiness. The Bodhisatta advises him to avoid greed and not let the pursuit of material wealth and success take over his life. He believes that "wickedness and greed" are two major barriers to achieving holiness. Instead, he stresses the importance of prioritizing the needs of others and leading a life of moderation and self-control to attain true holiness.

While not directly stated, Bodhisatta's words of warning appear to reference behaviors commonly associated with malevolence, which bear a notable likeness to those displayed by individuals diagnosed with antisocial personality disorder, also referred to as psychopathy or sociopathy. This disorder is marked by an absence of regard for societal norms and others' emotions, often leading to impulsive and unapologetic behaviors, including criminal acts. The Bodhisatta's admonitions serve as a preventative measure against such actions. It is important to acknowledge that the term "psychopath" carries a negative stigma and can be linked to traits like cruelty, heartlessness, and manipulation. As a result, it is wise to refrain from using this term, as it has the potential to marginalize individuals who have been diagnosed with mental health conditions (Patrick, 2022). It is also worth mentioning that the definition of "psychopath" has undergone changes over time and may not always be used exclusively in a clinical context. Psychopathy is a mental illness that leads individuals to exhibit behaviors that can be harmful to others or society. Despite its stigmatizing connotations, the term "psychopathy" is often used interchangeably with personality disorder to describe the associated actions. It is worth noting that psychopathy should not be mistaken for sociopathy, and it is important to differentiate between the two. Personality disorders are a group of conditions, which include psychopathic disorders, that can have a profound impact on a person's social behavior in three crucial areas: self-presentation, perception by others, and response to the recognition of their disorder. Those with psychopathic disorders often find it challenging to form meaningful relationships with others and may struggle to empathize with their emotions. Furthermore, they may show indications of criminal behavior and may not take responsibility for their actions.

Individuals with psychopathic tendencies are often capable of concealing their condition and presenting themselves as "average" to those around them. Such individuals are typically cautious in their behavior, striving to conform to social norms and avoid drawing attention to their symptoms. As a result, people with an antisocial personality disorder or psycho-pathic tendencies may come across as self-assured, congenial, and stable despite their inability to empathize with others and their tendency to manipulate those around them to achieve their objectives (Patrick, 2022). Identifying individuals with psychopathic traits can be a difficult task as they are often adept at concealing their true nature. However, upon closer examination of their behavior and attitude, it becomes evident that they may be merely putting on a façade. Such individuals have often been associated with turbulent relationships, unlawful actions, and disregard for societal norms. Additionally, individuals with psychopathy often struggle to establish genuine connections with others due to their limited capacity for empathy. The disorder was initially diagnosed through the use of sixteen criteria developed by Cleckley, an American psychiatrist, in 1976. These criteria assess psychological stability (including qualities such as charm and likability), deviant behavior (such as impulsiveness and irresponsibility), and impaired affect and social connectedness (such as a lack of empathy, no remorse for harming others, and manipulative and deceptive tendencies). It is important to note that not all individuals with psychopathy display violent or dangerous behavior, which contradicts the warnings of the Bodhisatta. However, it is crucial to acknowledge that the conduct that is typical of a diagnosis of psychopathic tendencies inevitably results in both personal and interpersonal distress (Fisher & Hany, 2021). In certain circumstances, individuals exhibiting such tendencies may be unaware of the harm they have caused or may struggle to regulate their actions. Thus, it is essential to identify indicators of psychopathy and offer assistance to those impacted.

The diagnostic criteria and symptoms of psychopathy have undergone changes in accordance with the DSM's definitions. The term "psychopathy" has been replaced by "antisocial personality disorder," which now encompasses conduct and behavioral abnormalities in childhood, along with other previously identified traits (APA, 2013). The connection between this shift and the Bodhisatta's cautionary advice in the story is that individuals with antisocial personality disorder may display multiple behaviors that hinder the attainment of spiritual purity. Antisocial behavior is characterized by actions that cause harm to interpersonal relationships. In contrast to prosocial behaviors such as helping or volunteering, antisocial actions involve dishonesty and manipulation to achieve personal goals, as noted by Fisher and Hany in 2021. Individuals with Antisocial Personality Disorder may exhibit manipulative or deceitful behavior, act impulsively without considering the effects on others, and may encounter difficulties in maintaining healthy relationships. In addition to struggling with anger and aggression, they may also be more prone to engaging in criminal behavior.

In this situation, it seems that the teachings of the Bodhisatta are particularly applicable. While it is not accurate to say that those with antisocial personality disorder are inherently selfish or lacking in empathy, the values of greed and disregard for others that can be associated with the disorder are not in line with Bodhisatta's teachings. Instead, the Bodhisatta advocates for a life of kindness, compassion, and empathy, even in challenging circumstances. Furthermore, the Bodhisatta encourages acts of generosity and respect for others, even when they may not be reciprocated. Therefore, it is advised to steer clear of the path of the antisocial person and follow the Bodhisatta's teachings. While only a small percentage of the population receives a diagnosis of antisocial personality disorder, it can be challenging to determine the true prevalence of this condition. This is because many individuals do not seek treatment for such behaviors. As a result, it is likely that more people suffer from this disorder than currently reported. Moreover, not all instances of antisocial behavior are indicative of a mental disorder, which makes identifying those who require specialized care even more challenging. Treating personality disorders can be a challenging task, as many individuals perceive their symptoms as integral aspects of their identity (Millon et al., 2011; John et al., 2008). As a result, seeking treatment may not be a top priority, and if treatment is pursued, adherence to therapy may be lacking. Moreover, the presentation of personality disorder symptoms can be easily mistaken for typical behavior, posing obstacles to accurate diagnosis and effective intervention. Hence, it is crucial to approach the matter with compassion and comprehension. Attentively hearing out their apprehensions, acknowledging their emotions, and demonstrating genuine concern for their welfare are all vital measures in providing the necessary support. Displaying empathy fosters a secure and reliable atmosphere where everyone can collaborate toward a resolution. Additionally, it is advisable to furnish them with assistance and resources to help them manage the diagnosis. In due course, we will delve further into the treatment of personality disorders.

Antisocial Personality Disorder and Extreme Violence

The Cula-Dhammapala-jataka (Ja 358) is a story that portrays characters exhibiting symptoms associated with antisocial personality disorders. In the story, Queen Canda and her son, Bodhisatta Dhammapala, are subjected to violent treatment. One day, while playing with her son, the queen failed to greet the king as he arrived at her residence. This enraged the king, who feared that the baby would eventually become more important than him, as evidenced by the queen's disregard for his presence. Accordingly, he ordered that the baby be executed. It was extremely upsetting for the queen, and she begged the executioner to spare him. Nevertheless, he snatched the boy from her arms and severed his hands, feet, and finally, his head. Eventually, the queen became ill with grief and died.

Although mental disorders are not explicitly mentioned in this story, the actions of the king and executioner suggest extreme forms of psychopathy and antisocial personality disorder. Antisocial personality disorder is characterized by a lack of empathy, which is evident in the king's willingness to condone violence and the executioner's readiness to carry out orders without remorse. Such behavior can have serious consequences for those affected. It is difficult to imagine committing such violent acts without recognizing the harm being done, indicating a lack of empathy. Research shows that antisocial personality disorder is more prevalent in men than women (Hare, 2003; Lilienfeld & Widows, 2005).

The relationship between violence and mental illness is complex and multifaceted, with many nuances to consider. While certain mental health conditions may increase the likelihood of being victimized, exposure to violence can also lead to mental health challenges. Despite media depictions that often inaccurately associate mental illness with erratic or violent behavior, even those with conditions that may exhibit such behaviors do not necessarily act aggressively. Rather, aggression is more commonly influenced by factors such as substance abuse, economic disadvantage, and social marginalization.

Research has demonstrated that substances that influence the brain and central nervous system can heighten aggression and violence (Lindqvist & Allebeck, 1990). For instance, the use of alcohol, cocaine, amphetamines, hallucinogens, PCP, or ecstasy may raise the levels of baseline violence in some individuals (Rueve & Welton, 2008). Additionally, the cessation of specific substances like alcohol, heroin, and certain sedatives may increase an individual's likelihood of engaging in violent behavior.

Although it is unclear whether the king and his men were subject to any physical alterations, it is evident that the king was possessed by a deep-seated fear of losing his grip on power. When an individual reconfigures their brain's reward circuits to derive pleasure from fulfilling their desire for power, it can become an addiction (Al-Rodhan, 2014; Di Chiara & Bassareo, 2007). Hence, it is possible that the king experienced initial signs of withdrawal when faced with the prospect of losing his "fix" - control and authority - which may have heightened his inclination towards violent behavior.

Furthermore, it is crucial to acknowledge that linking mental health with violence can have negative consequences and exacerbate the social stigma faced by those with mental illness (Rueve & Welton, 2008). Studies indicate that individuals with mental illness are more vulnerable to becoming targets of violence rather than being the ones perpetrating it (Maniglio, 2009). As a result, those without mental disorders may be more inclined to act violently towards individuals who display behaviors that are deemed abnormal or potentially dangerous, even if such behaviors do not signify any genuine threat of harm (such as shouting or exhibiting inappropriate emotional reactions).

Narcissistic Personality Disorder and Humanistic Therapy

There are similarities between antisocial personality disorder and narcissistic personality disorder, which we will delve into shortly. In the Kama-jataka (Ja 467), there is a tale of a young man who becomes a viceroy and finds the position unsatisfying. He dreams of seizing the kingdom and ruling it himself. The king's brother grants him rule over the kingdom to appease his desire for power, but his greed only grows. One kingdom is not enough, and he soon desires two, then three. His thirst for power cannot be quenched. After witnessing Sakka succumb to greed, the Bodhisatta devised a plan reminiscent of a prior event. Sakka proposed three thriving cities for the king to conquer, only to vanish when the king mobilized a caravan to find them. Meanwhile, Sakka became sickly, prompting the wise teacher Bodhisatta to advise him that his greed was the root cause of his ailment. The Bodhisatta further explained how living a life driven by desire can lead to physical and mental afflictions.

It appears that this individual may be exhibiting symptoms of narcissistic personality disorder. This disorder is characterized by a variety of traits, including reactive anger, exhibitionism, entitlement, and a need for admiration. These traits can be observed in the patient's behavior, as evidenced by their tendency to exaggerate their accomplishments and disregard the feelings of others. Furthermore, individuals with this personality disorder may exhibit a lack of empathy and a feeling of entitlement. As a result, forming meaningful relationships can be challenging for them. Narcissistic Personality Disorder shares a common trait with Antisocial Personality Disorder: a lack of empathy. According to research, approximately 6% of the general population may develop this disorder at some point in their lives (Stinson et al., 2008). Unfortunately, the consequences can be severe, including depression, substance abuse, and social isolation. Fortunately, there are numerous treatment options available, such as psychotherapy, medication, and lifestyle changes.

One of the most challenging aspects of comprehending and addressing narcissistic personality disorder is the overreliance on behavioral observation and self-esteem evaluations, as noted by Miller et al. (2007). Insufficient specific criteria exist to justify the diagnosis of this disorder, despite other scholars, such as Ronningstam (2011), outlining more detailed criteria. There are certain diagnostic traits called diagnostic trait facets that include: grandiosity (meaning an exaggerated or unrealistic sense of superiority and capability), variable self-esteem (which means alternating between overconfidence and insecurity), reactions to perceived threats to self-esteem (such as feeling humiliated when criticized or experiencing failure), self-enhancing interpersonal behavior (which includes excessive admiration and attention seeking), self-serving interpersonal behavior (which means having an expectation of unreasonable rights and services), avoidance (which means being internally self-sufficient and distant from others), aggression (which includes overtly expressed or internally concealed interpersonal argumentative and hostile attitudes), perfectionism (which means having exceptionally high and inflexible standards for oneself or others), and impaired empathic ability (which is compromised by self-centeredness and self-serving interests; Ronningstam, 2011).

It is difficult to determine with certainty whether the king in the story possessed any of these traits, but we can make inferences based on his behavior. For instance, he displayed an insatiable need for power that may have stemmed from an exaggerated need for admiration, which is a characteristic of narcissistic personality disorder. Furthermore, his desire to expand his rule could be a sign of his grandiose attitude and self-serving interpersonal behavior. He may have believed that he was superior and capable of ruling over numerous kingdoms, and his self-serving attitude may have led him to believe that he had an uncontestable right to rule over them.

Furthermore, this narrative offers a glimpse into the king's conduct following the disappointment of not acquiring additional territories. His physical malady is severe, perhaps indicating a response to a perceived challenge to his self-worth. A person with narcissistic inclinations may experience profound shame and apprehension when confronted with failure or the possibility of it. This could imply that the king is grappling with narcissistic personality disorder and that his anguish may impel him to pursue medical attention, even if it pertains primarily to his physical health.

In the story, the Bodhisatta employs classic psychotherapy techniques to overcome his ailments. While the specifics of how he counsels the king are not described, it is evident that the healing occurs by addressing the king's psychological behavior, which is essentially psychotherapy. Modern approaches like humanistic or person-centered therapy could potentially benefit the king. Additionally, the Bodhisatta may have used cognitive-behavioral therapy, which aims to help clients identify and alter their thought patterns and behaviors. Adopting this approach could aid in the king's quest to tackle the underlying cause of his affliction, paving the way for enduring transformation. As per this method, mental health concerns are a result of a person's actions being in conflict with their genuine self (Boettcher et al., 2022). Humanistic therapy is founded on the principle that individuals possess an inherent desire to evolve, develop, and unlock their maximum potential. This type of therapy centers on the individual's personal experience, emphasizing their emotions and principles, and their aptitude to make sound judgments and choices. Its objective is to create a secure and encouraging environment for patients to reach their full potential, unearth their self-value, explore their identity, and act in a way that supports and reinforces what they have discovered.

In this tale, the wise Bodhisatta had the ability to present the situation in a manner that would boost the king's confidence and potential. The Bodhisatta could have appealed to the king's natural inclination towards leadership, a role that is essential to the king's self-esteem. By reframing the situation, the Bodhisatta could have suggested that taking on too much responsibility might impede the king's ability to be an exceptional leader. Instead, the key to becoming a great leader may lie in ruling over a few select territories with excellence and acclaim. This is one example of a modern therapeutic technique that could be quite effective, but there are other forms of therapy (which will be discussed later in this chapter) that could also benefit the king.

A noteworthy attribute of humanistic therapy that has been found to be efficacious is the therapist's display of unconditional positive regard (Boettcher et al., 2022). Essentially, this means the therapist must maintain a non-judgmental stance towards everything the patient expresses. No matter the nature of the patient's discourse, the therapist refrains from reprimanding or criticizing them, fostering an atmosphere where patients can actualize their full potential and attain self-realization.

The Bodhisatta provided wise counsel to the king and did so without any hint of judgment. Rather, he conveyed that a life of excess and indulgence would not lead to fulfillment or spiritual enlightenment. In today's context, the Bodhisatta's guidance might align with humanistic therapy, which emphasizes the importance of being one's best self. Ultimately, the Bodhisatta's aim was to help the king achieve his full potential by promoting balance and moderation. Bodhisatta sought to guide the king towards a life of greater purpose and significance by steering him towards a more spiritual path.

Narcissistic Personality Disorder and Cognitive-Behavioral Therapy

In the Kamanita-jataka (Ja 228), there is a tale of a king who indulges in his desire for wealth, sex, and greed, and rules unjustly. Seeing this, the Bodhisatta, who is reborn as Sakka, comes up with a plan. Disguised as a young man, he approaches the king and tells him about three prosperous cities that he could conquer. The king expresses interest and agrees to follow the young man with his armies the next day. However, Sakka returns to heaven and stays unseen for several days.

The king and his army scoured the land in search of him, but alas, their efforts proved fruitless. The king was overcome with grief and anguish, his physical health suffering greatly as a result. He mourned the missed opportunity to bask in the glory of conquering those cities. One day, Sakka, in his Bodhisatta form, came upon the king in his state of despair and offered his assistance. The king was hesitant, having received no relief from any other healer in the kingdom. But the Bodhisatta persisted, asking the king to reveal the source of his affliction. The king admitted that the loss of the three cities had contributed to his illness. From there, the Bodhisatta sought to guide the king towards a new perspective on desire and its pitfalls.

While not overtly addressing psychological conditions, it's possible to draw parallels between the king in this tale and the narcissistic ruler in the Kama-jataka (Ja 467). These similarities suggest that many monarchs may exhibit symptoms of narcissistic personality disorder, such as grandiose thinking and self-centered conduct (De Brito et al., 2021).

The Bodhisatta aimed to shift the king's perspective on power and desire, guiding him towards a healthier, more adaptive mindset. This approach bears resemblance to a widely practiced form of therapy known as cognitive-behavioral therapy (CBT). CBT targets negative thought patterns and behaviors that do not align with an individual's lifestyle or environment, helping them to make positive changes. Cognitive Behavioral Therapy (CBT) places emphasis on recognizing, comprehending, and altering negative thought processes, behaviors, and emotional patterns. It operates on the principle that our thoughts, emotions, and actions are interwoven and that modifying one component can lead to positive effects on the others. Interestingly, the Bodhisatta employed this very approach when assisting the king. It is crucial to first recognize any negative thinking patterns before applying a cognitive-behavioral framework to treat the monarch. For instance, the king may harbor a belief that states, "Without dominion over those three prosperous cities as foretold, I will perish or diminish in significance." Such a thought process is considered maladaptive, as it is impractical to aspire for global domination. Hence, fostering acceptance of this notion would serve as a fundamental approach towards a favorable treatment outcome.

The next step is to recognize the negative emotions that stem from these thoughts. For instance, the king may feel fear, anxiety, or dread due to the possibility of not ruling enough. This emotion can lead to maladaptive behaviors, which is the subsequent step in CBT. The king's actions may be a response to a perceived threat to his power, such as an untreatable illness. However, it's important to note that illness is not a behavior but rather a physiological reaction to the threat of losing power, which is the body's natural response to its environment. According to Cheng et al. (2013), individuals with narcissistic tendencies are more likely to experience heightened physiological stress responses in everyday situations compared to those without. Given the circumstances, it's understandable that the king would have a strong reaction to the threat at hand. Our bodies naturally initiate a stress response to protect ourselves against perceived dangers. Therefore, the king's illness could be a physical manifestation of his fear of losing command and influence in a situation that's beyond his control. This is a typical reaction for people who exhibit narcissistic traits.

Enmeshment of Family Structures

In the Culla-Palobhana-jataka (Ja 263), the Bodhisatta is portrayed as a Queen's son who faced a unique challenge during infancy. Despite being calm in the presence of a man, he refused to feed from a woman's breast. This led to 16 years of no exposure to women or knowledge of life's pleasures. Concerned about his son's future, the king searched for a young lady who could seduce the Bodhisatta, marry him, and introduce him to the pleasures of life.

Ultimately, this strategy worked, and the Bodhisatta succumbed to the allure of women.

The Bodhisatta's upbringing was marked by the trappings of privilege and indulgence, which may have concealed a deeper psychological harm. His parents strived to shield him from all adversity, leaving him with limited avenues for personal growth and discovery. Such a restricted environment could have left a lasting imprint on his psyche, akin to the effects of child abuse. As an adult, the Bodhisatta may struggle with emotional intimacy due to these early experiences. This narrative highlights how a particular family developed their own unique dynamics that deviated from conventional societal, cultural, and biological expectations. First and foremost, it is important to examine the concept of familial norms or family structures - the unwritten rules that dictate how family members interact. Scholars refer to this as an "invisible code" that guides family dynamics (Minuchin, 1974). Various factors, such as gender roles, hierarchical relationships, and expectations for behavior, can influence the coding of this family structure. Essentially, this structure is like a rulebook that fosters stability within the family unit. It is evident that this particular family, along with their servants, established an exceptional family structure that would have been unconventional for its time and still would be today. Such families and their dynamic arrangements are indeed uncommon.

Psychologists have observed that family dynamics can play a significant role in the development of psychological disorders. When family members are overly enmeshed, meaning they lack clear boundaries and function as a single unit, it can hinder individual autonomy and ultimately lead to a decline in psychological wellbeing. This lack of independence can also make it difficult to adapt to changes in the family or environment, leading to a lack of resilience.

Prolonged Grief Disorder

The Kesava-jataka (Ja 346) features a prominent character who is described as having a "mental disorder." The story follows the Bodhisatta, who is reincarnated into a Brahmin family and goes by the name Kappa. As a child, Kappa embraced a religious lifestyle and formed a close bond with another ascetic named Kesava. The two were even described as being "intimate" with each other. On one occasion, Kesava joined some other ascetics on a trip to Benares to procure salt and vinegar. While there, they were invited to spend time in the king's garden, where they were generously fed and provided with accommodations.

After spending some time in the garden, Kesava expressed a desire to leave. However, the king kindly asked him to stay since he was an old man and could send younger ascetics back to the Himalayas. While Kesava remained in the garden alone, Kappa returned to the Himalayas with the other ascetics. Kesava struggled to sleep and eat properly as he missed Kappa, which eventually led to an internal illness affecting his ability to digest food.

Upon realizing his illness, the king promptly sent him back to the serene Himalayas. In the presence of Kappa Kesava, the affliction dissipated and the king was able to relish life once more. Kesava offered nourishment, which further improved the king's well-being. When inquired about the cure for his ailment, the king attributed it to the affection of his dear friend. In light of Kesava's absence causing the mental disorder, it is worth examining how contemporary medicine would diagnose this behavior. According to the DSM-5, there are specific diagnostic criteria for persistent complex bereavement disorder, also known as prolonged grief disorder (APA, 2013). This classification indicates that clinical psychologists and practitioners acknowledge that grief responses can resemble mental disorders. The typical grief response has been compared to a traumatic injury to the brain, the body's stress systems, and its emotional regulation systems (Schut et al., 1991). This disruption of normal functioning can result in a range of psychological and physiological symptoms that may mimic those of major depression, anxiety disorders, and post-traumatic stress disorder (PTSD).

The behavior exhibited by Kesava in this story aligns with the diagnostic criteria for prolonged grief disorder. Such criteria include a persistent desire for a deceased or lost loved one, which can be both distressing and painful for the individual. Additionally, individuals with this disorder may struggle greatly to accept the loss, experience feelings of meaninglessness, harbor bitterness towards the loss, and find it difficult to engage in new activities. It is worth noting that for these symptoms to meet pathological standards, they must persist for at least six months following the death, as noted by Bonnano et al. (2002) and Prigerson et al. (2009). According to research, grieving for more than six months can have lasting negative effects such as sleep disturbances, cardiovascular issues, and problems with work and relationships (Bryant et al., 1996). While it is unclear how long Kesava experienced these symptoms, they were severe enough to cause harm and concern among those close to him.

Kesava's experience is distinct in that his friend Kappa, while alive, is presently absent and distant from him, eliciting a profound sense of grief. This phenomenon, known as ambiguous loss in psychology (Boss, 2010), describes the loss of someone who is still alive, yet may be absent either psychologically or physically. Ambiguous loss can be a challenging form of grief to navigate, as it does not follow the same clear path as more traditional types of loss. It can leave you feeling stuck in a sort of limbo, with no clear way to move forward. One common example of this type of loss is when a family member begins to exhibit advanced symptoms of dementia or other memory loss disorders. Though the person is still present, there is a sense that their personality and psychology may never fully return to what it once was. Kesava may have experienced a profound emotional reaction due to his unwavering belief that he would never reunite with Kappa. This resulted in an intense state of grief that could be likened to the sorrow experienced after death. This type of grief can be particularly challenging to comprehend since it is not as widely recognized as typical grief caused by death (Boss, 2010).

The Sujata-jataka (Ja 352) also illustrates grief as a mental disorder. The story follows the Bodhisatta, who is the son of a landowner named Sujata. When Sujata's grandfather passed away, his father was deeply affected and struggled with grief for a prolonged period. In his garden, he created a beautiful memorial using the remains of his beloved late father. During his regular visits, he lovingly adorned the memorial with delicate flowers. However, on certain occasions, when he would visit the burial site, he would refrain from partaking in basic personal hygiene and business activities. Such behavior is often linked to an atypical grief response, which can result in a persistent sense of loss known as "ambiguous loss" (Prigerson et al., 2009). Individuals experiencing ambiguous loss may often feel burdened and may suffer from depression or anxiety.

The Bodhisatta's enlightening approach becomes the cure for his father's ailment. By feeding a deceased ox, he shows his father the futility of fretting over the departed. This method shares similarities with cognitive-behavioral therapy, which was previously discussed in regard to managing narcissistic personality disorder. In fact, studies have shown that grief-focused cognitive-behavioral therapy is a successful remedy for prolonged grief disorder (Bryant et al., 2014). While cognitive-behavioral therapy can be effective on its own for treating prolonged grief disorder, incorporating exposure therapy can further enhance its effectiveness. By implementing grief-focused cognitive-behavioral therapy alongside exposure therapy, patients can maximize the benefits of treatment. Exposure therapy requires patients to confront the source of their distress, such as anxiety or sadness caused by the death of a loved one. Patients undergoing this therapy can learn to manage emotions related to their trauma, leading to improved mental health and a more positive outlook on life.

Research has shown that those who receive cognitive-behavioral therapy combined with revisiting their emotions about the death are more likely to see improvement in their symptoms compared to those who only receive CBT (Bryant et al., 1996). This highlights the importance of frequently facing the reality of death. It's interesting to note how Bodhisatta utilized the dead oxen to help his father undergo cognitive-behavioral therapy. By observing the oxen, the father was able to recognize his own maladaptive thoughts and eventually overcome his grief through therapy. This process allowed him to identify and address the emotions and behaviors that were holding him back.

Another intriguing and complex aspect of the Jataka stories is that the Bodhisatta, in other tales, attempts to normalize discussions about death. Although this particular batch does not depict it, the Bodhisatta's teachings, as well as those of Buddhism today, emphasize that death is an inevitable aspect of life that should not be feared, dreaded, or lamented. The Bodhisatta's acceptance of death during his past life may have contributed to the effectiveness of cognitive-behavioral therapy in this story. This psychological technique encourages individuals to acknowledge, reframe, and ultimately accept their thoughts and emotions. The lesson of accepting death as a natural part of life, taught by the Bodhisatta, may have positively impacted his mental wellbeing, leading him to make wise decisions and ultimately achieve enlightenment.

The Ghatapandita-jataka (Ja 454) contains several smaller narratives, one of which relates to the topic of psychological disorders, namely, the death of one of King Vasudeva's beloved sons. Following his son's death, the king fell into a state of deep sorrow and neglected all of his daily duties, spending his days in bed mourning. Concerned for his brother's well-being, Ghatapandita feigned insanity, crying out for a hare. The city soon began to speculate that Ghatapandita had lost his mind and was no longer in his right state of mind.

The plan worked, and the king was curious as to why his brother was fixated on acquiring a hare. When he inquired, Ghatapandita upped the ante and asked for a hare made of precious gems and even the moon itself! The king was convinced that his brother had lost his mind, but Ghatapandita used these exaggerated requests to show the king how his own excessive grief was making him appear equally irrational. The king claimed that this realization helped ease his sorrow.

This narrative bears many similarities to the Sujata-jataka, both in terms of the emotional responses displayed by the protagonist's family and the method employed to alleviate their suffering. By utilizing the same approach as that outlined in the previous tale, Ghatapandita was able to assist his brother in overcoming his distress via grief-focused cognitive-behavioral therapy. As a result, Ghatapandita's brother was able to pinpoint his own unhelpful thoughts (such as "the loss of my child is intolerable") by identifying those of his brothers (such as the availability of jewel hares and the moon). This realization enabled the king to recognize the negative feeling that had resulted from his thought pattern (excessive and debilitating grief), allowing him to modify his unhelpful behavior.

Sex and Love Addiction

The Kunala-jataka (Ja 536) contains several brief stories that aim to caution against the perils of women. One story depicts a woman who exhibits signs of an addiction to sex or love. In this tale, a king's daughter seeks a husband, and five suitors, including the Bodhisatta and his brothers, vie for her hand. The young woman ends up falling in love with all five men and marries them all. She also engages in a secret affair with a disabled servant while her husbands are away.

In private, she promises all six of her lovers that they will become king after her father's death. When her husbands learn of her infidelity, they all lose their love for her and abandon her to pursue an ascetic life.

This woman exhibits symptoms consistent with what may be diagnosed as an excessive sex addiction. Manifestations of compulsive sexual behavior are apparent, including participation in risky and unhealthy sexual activities despite adverse outcomes, as well as utilizing sexual encounters as a coping mechanism for managing stress and anxiety. Furthermore, she demonstrates a lack of control over her impulses and an inability to discontinue the behavior, even when she expresses a desire to do so. Unlike substance addiction, sex addiction remains a subject of considerable controversy. In the DSM-5, hypersexuality is explained as distinct from sex addiction due to the latter's elusive definition (Hall, 2011). Both terms, however, denote an elevated or excessive level of sexual activity, a descriptor fitting for the woman in question. Hypersexuality encompasses not only heightened libido but also compulsive behavioral patterns that disrupt daily functioning. This includes an inability to regulate sexual urges, even when such regulation is desired, and can result in significant repercussions such as relational conflicts, financial hardships, and legal entanglements.

The contemporary landscape presents a myriad of manifestations for sex addiction, rendering its precise definition challenging. For instance, individuals may perceive sex addiction as synonymous with compulsive engagement in Internet pornography, thereby experiencing distress over the perceived necessity to consume copious amounts of such content (Hall, 2011). Furthermore, persistent sexual fantasies and preoccupations may encumber the individual, impeding the fulfillment of routine daily obligations and instigating distress. The woman depicted in the narrative exemplifies potential symptoms of sex addiction, as evidenced by her pursuit of multiple partners—five husbands and a sixth lover—evidently driven by a compulsive need to satiate her sexual desires.

Research has shown that sexual satisfaction can be addictive due to its impact on the brain's reward systems and the release of dopamine (Robbins & Everitt, 2010). This can lead to a strong dependence on the pleasure of sexual satisfaction, potentially resulting in compulsive behavior. The ramifications of such behavior encompass a spectrum of physical and psychological afflictions, including but not limited to depression, anxiety, and interpersonal discord. It is plausible that the woman portrayed in the narrative harbored intentions to terminate her liaison with the sixth lover, as this act constituted a breach of fidelity; however, her inability to curb her impulses suggests a lack of control over her desires. Moreover, it is conceivable that pre-existing cognitive distortions surrounding sexual behavior influenced her decision to enter into multiple marriages. Notably, scholarly literature posits a correlation between childhood adversity and subsequent maladaptive behaviors or relational patterns in adulthood (Fisher, 2007; Bechara & Damasio, 2002). Consequently, the woman's narrative potentially exemplifies the trajectory wherein unresolved childhood trauma precipitates maladaptive conduct in later life. Furthermore, it underscores the formidable nature of desires and the challenges inherent in their regulation.

It's possible that the woman also struggled with love addiction, which can be even more difficult to diagnose and treat than sex addiction due to its manifestation as hypersexuality. Love addiction is often described as "immature love" by researchers because it is characterized by maladaptive social interactions. For instance, maladaptive relationships may involve power, possession, overprotection, pity, and perversion. Although we do not have all the details about the woman's background, it's possible that her desire for five husbands instead of one could be due to a misunderstanding of romantic love.

One of the defining characteristics of love addiction, which sets it apart from sex addiction, is the conviction that a romantic connection has the power to mend emotional traumas and barriers (Peele & Brodsky, 1992, pp. 144-157). This suggests that the individual is grappling with compulsive behavior that can potentially be resolved through cognitive-behavioral therapy, as previously mentioned. The initial step in assisting individuals experiencing distress due to sex or love addiction is identifying the maladaptive thoughts responsible for their emotions and behaviors. By pinpointing the thoughts causing the distress, cognitive-behavioral therapy can reframe and replace them with adaptive thoughts that promote healthier emotions and behaviors. This therapeutic approach is commonly employed to help individuals struggling with addiction.

Psychosis and Schizophrenia

The Maha-ummagga-jataka (Ja 546) offers insight into psychological conditions through its portrayal of characters revealing their hidden secrets. In one instance, a character confesses to having a hidden wound on their skin, while another admits to stealing valuable possessions from the king. However, one individual shares a particularly concerning detail - on holy days, they experience possession by a goblin and bark uncontrollably. Without proper context, this behavior could be interpreted as a symptom of psychosis.

Psychosis is a symptom of psychotic disorders such as schizophrenia and can have devastating effects on individuals (Barch, 2022). These conditions can impact a person's emotional health, social relationships, and professional life, as they are often accompanied by delusions (which we will explore in a separate chapter) and hallucinations. While the symptoms may appear alike, they are, in fact, distinct from each other. Delusions are beliefs that persist despite contradictory evidence, whereas hallucinations are sensory experiences that occur without any external stimulation. As a result, hallucinations arise when individuals perceive things that do not actually exist in the real world (Barch, 2022). Hallucinations can affect any of the five senses and are often associated with mental health disorders such as schizophrenia. While they can stem from mental illness, such as schizophrenia, they can also stem from physical illness or medication. Delusions come in two categories, primary delusions, and secondary delusions, depending on whether they are held by an individual alone or by others as well. Depending on the type of hallucination, it may be visual, auditory, olfactory, or tactile. Hallucinations can be unsettling and disruptive, and can hinder everyday life.

The effect of these disorders on an individual's life can be quite severe when one imagines the experience. A tale is told of a man who was believed to be possessed by a goblin, howling like a frenzied dog. During that era, such behavior was deemed abnormal and a potential sign of psychosis. It is noteworthy that even today, such actions would lead others to believe that the individual is experiencing a psychotic episode.

Hallucinations can manifest through any of the five senses. In cases of psychosis, individuals may perceive smells, sounds, tastes, sights, or even physical sensations that are not actually present (Barch, 2022). For instance, they may see an entity that is not really there or feel something creeping on their skin. To be diagnosed with schizophrenia, an individual must display at least two of the following symptoms for a minimum of one month: hallucinations, delusions, disordered speech, extremely disordered or catatonic behavior, and negative symptoms (APA, 2013). Schizoaffective disorder, delusional disorder, and brief psychotic disorder share similarities (Yoon-Sun et al., 2021). Based on the story, it's possible that the man featured suffered from disorders related to schizophrenia, and treatment options were limited at the time. Even today, psychotherapy is often used alongside antipsychotic medications to treat psychosis or schizophrenia, as it provides valuable insight and support that medication alone cannot. Given the novelty of these medications, it's unclear how individuals with severe mental health issues were treated in the past.

Conclusion

The Jataka stories are a treasure trove of ancient Buddhist literature that offer valuable insights into the human psyche. These tales showcase a diverse range of characters who exhibit psychological symptoms consistent with various mental disorders. As such, analyzing the characters in the

Psychological Disorder: Mental Health Challenges

Jataka stories using the latest diagnostic criteria from the DSM-5 can provide significant insights into the human mind.

In this chapter, we delve into the psychological symptoms displayed by the characters in the Jataka stories and explore how these symptoms align with the diagnostic criteria found within the DSM-5. The DSM-5 encompasses a broad spectrum of disorders, including but not limited to personality disorders, psychotic and schizophrenia-related disorders, substance use disorders, and mood disorders. Through a thorough analysis of the characters' actions, we can gain insight into which DSM-5 disorders are most applicable to their individual experiences.

While a formal diagnosis would require more detailed information than what is available in the jataka stories, it is still valuable to contemplate the behaviors displayed by these historical figures and ponder how they might be approached in modern times. Mental health experts can leverage these tales to assist individuals in comprehending their own emotional challenges and offer beneficial guidance on how to manage them. Moreover, these accounts can function as a tool to improve awareness and understanding of mental health issues and promote empathy for those who are experiencing mental illness.

Contemplating the Jataka stories allows us to recognize the strides we have made as a society in comprehending the intricacies of human psychology. When we contrast how we approach these behaviors today versus in the past, we can gain insight into our progress. Moreover, these tales can inspire empathy and kindness towards individuals who are grappling with mental health issues. Ultimately, the Jataka stories offer a meaningful perspective for comprehending and appreciating the human condition.

References

Al-Rodhan, N. (2014). The neurochemistry of power: Implications for political change. *The Oxford University Politics Blog.* https://blog.politics.ox.ac.uk/neurochemistry-power-implications-political-change/

American Psychiatric Association. (2013). *Diagnostic and statistical manual of mental disorders* (5th ed.). American Psychiatric Publishing.

Barch, D. M. (2022). Schizophrenia spectrum disorders. In R. Biswas-Diener & E. Diener (Eds.), *Noba textbook series: Psychology.* DEF publishers. http://noba.to/5d98nsy4

Bechara, A., & Damasio, H. (2002). Decision-making and addiction (part 1): Impaired motivation of somatic states in substance dependent individuals when pondering decisions with negative future consequences. *Neuropsychologia, 40*(2), 1675–1689.

Boettcher, H., Hofmann, S. G., & Wu, Q. J. (2022). Therapeutic orientations. In R. Biswas-Diener & E. Diener (Eds.), *Noba textbook series: Psychology.* DEF publishers. http://noba.to/fjtnpwsk

Bonanno, G. A., Wortman, C. B., Lehman, D. R., Tweed, R. G., Haring, M., Sonnega, J., Carr, D., & Nesse, R. M. (2002). Resilience to loss and chronic grief: A prospective study from preloss to 18-months postloss. *Journal of Personality and Social Psychology, 83*(5), 1150–1164.

Boss, P. (2010). The trauma and complicated grief of ambiguous loss. *Pastoral Psychology, 59*(2), 137-145.

Bryant, R. A., Kenny, L., Joscelyne, A., Rawson, N., Maccallum, F., Cahill, C., Hopwood, S., Aderka, I., & Nickerson, A. (2014). Treating prolonged grief disorder: A randomized clinical trial. *JAMA Psychiatry*, 71(12), 1332-1339.

Carpenter, W. T., Jr., & Davis, J. M. (2012). Another view of the history of antipsychotic drug discovery and development. *Molecular Psychiatry*, 17(12), 1168–1173.

Cheng, J. T., Tracy, J. L., & Miller, G. E. (2013). Are narcissists hardy or vulnerable? The role of narcissism in the production of stress-related biomarkers in response to emotional distress. *Emotion*, 13(6), 1004–1011.

Cleckley, H. (1976). *The mask of sanity* (5th ed.). Mosby.

Crego, C., & Widiger, T. (2022). Personality disorders. In R. Biswas-Diener & E. Diener (Eds.), *Noba textbook series: Psychology*. DEF publishers. http://noba.to/67mvg5r2

De Brito, S. A., Forth, A. E., Baskin-Sommers, A. R., Brazil, I. A., Kimonis, E. R., Pardini, D., Fri ck, P. J., Blair, R. J. R., & Viding, E. (2021). *Psychopathy*. https://doi.org/10.1038/s41572-021-00282-1

Di Chiara, G., & Bassareo, V. (2007). Reward system and addiction: What dopamine does and doesn't do. *Current Opinion in Pharmacology*, 7(1), 69-76.

Farreras, I. G. (2022). History of mental illness. In R. Biswas-Diener & E. Diener (Eds.), *Noba textbook series: Psychology*. DEF publishers. http://noba.to/65w3s7ex

Fisher, J. (2007). *Addictions and trauma recovery*. Basic Books.

Fisher, K. A., & Hany, M. (2021). Antisocial personality disorder. In *StatPearls* [Internet]. StatPearls Publishing.

Green, R. J., & Werner, P. D. (1996). Intrusiveness and closeness-caregiving: Rethinking the concept of family "enmeshment." *Family Process*, 35(2), 115-136.

Hall, P. (2011). A biopsychosocial view of sex addiction. *Sexual and Relationship Therapy*, 26(3), 217-228.

Hare, R. D. (2003). *The Hare Psychopathy Checklist* (2nd ed.). Multi-Health Systems. (Original edition published in 1991)

John, O. P., Robins, R. W., & Pervin, L. A. (Eds.). (2008). *Handbook of personality: Theory and research* (3rd ed.). Guilford Press.

Lilienfeld, S. O., & Widows, M. R. (2005). *Psychopathic Personality Inventory-Revised* (PPI-R) professional manual. Psychological Assessment Resources.

Lindqvist, P., & Allebeck, P. (1990). Schizophrenia and assaultive behaviour: The role of alcohol and drug abuse. *Acta Psychiatrica Scandinavica*, 82(3), 191-195.

Maniglio, R. (2009). Severe mental illness and criminal victimization: A systematic review. *Acta Psychiatrica Scandinavica*, 119(3), 180-191.

Miller, J. D., Campbell, W. K., & Pilkonis, P. A. (2007). Narcissistic personality disorder: Relations with distress and functional impairment. *Comprehensive Psychiatry*, 48(2), 170–177.

Millon, T. (2011). Disorders of personality: *Introducing a DSM/ICD spectrum from normal to abnormal* (3rd ed.). John Wiley & Sons.

Minuchin, S. (1974). *Families & family therapy*. Harvard University Press.

Minuchin, S., Rosman, B. L., & Baker, L. (1978). *Psychosomatic families: Anorexia nervosa in context*. Harvard University Press.

Patrick, C. (2022). Psychopathy. In R. Biswas-Diener & E. Diener (Eds.), *Noba textbook series: Psychology*. DEF publishers. http://noba.to/ysg8mu9w

Peele, S., & Brodsky, A. (1992). *The truth about addiction and recovery*. Fireside.

Prigerson, H. G., Horowitz, M. J., Jacobs, S. C., Parkes, C. M., Aslan, M., Goodkin, K., Raphael, B., & Marwit, S. J. (2009). Prolonged grief disorder: Psychometric validation of criteria proposed for DSM-V and ICD-11. *PLoS Medicine*, 6(8), e100121.

Robbins, T., & Everitt, B. (Eds.). (2010). *The neurobiology of addiction*. Oxford University Press.

Ronningstam, E. (2011). Narcissistic personality disorder in DSM-V—in support of retaining a significant diagnosis. *Journal of Personality Disorders*, 25(2), 248-259.

Rueve, M. E., & Welton, R. S. (2008). Violence and mental illness. *Psychiatry (Edgmont)*, 5(5), 34-48.

Schultze-Lutter, F., Schmidt, S. J., & Theodoridou, A. (2018). Psychopathology—a precision tool in need of re-sharpening. *Frontiers in Psychiatry*, 9, 446.

Schut, H., de Keijser, J., van den Bout, J., & Dijkhuis, J. (1991). Post-traumatic stress symptoms in the first years of conjugal bereavement. *Anxiety Research*, 4(3), 225–234.

Stinson, F. S., Dawson, D. A., Goldstein, R. B., Chou, S. P., Huang, B., Smith, S. M., et al. (2008). Prevalence, correlates, disability, and comorbidity of DSM-IV narcissistic personality disorder: Results from the wave 2 national epidemiologic survey on alcohol and related conditions. *Journal of Clinical Psychiatry*, 69(7), 1033–1045.

Strickland, C. M., Drislane, L. E., Lucy, M., Krueger, R. F., & Patrick, C. J. (2013). Characterizing psychopathy using DSM-5 personality traits. *Assessment*, 20(3), 327-338.

Sussman, S. (2010). Love addiction: Definition, etiology, treatment. *Sexual Addiction & Compulsivity*, 17(1), 31-45.

Yoon-Sun, J., Young-Eun, K., & Seok-Jun, Y. (2021). The prevalence, incidence, and admission rate of diagnosed schizophrenia spectrum disorders in Korea, 2008–2017: A nationwide population-based study using claims big data analysis. *PLoS One*, 16(8), e0256221.

Zeanah, C. H., & Gleason, M. M. (2010). Reactive attachment disorder: A review for DSM-V. In American Psychiatric Association (Ed.), *DSM-V*. Washington, DC: American Psychiatric Association.

CHAPTER FIVE

SEXUALITY: EXPLORING HUMAN RELATIONSHIPS AND IDENTITY IN JATAKA STORIES

Introduction

The topic of human sexuality is a multifaceted aspect of life, particularly for humans. Different cultures and personal experiences have contributed to the various interpretations of sexuality, and these understandings are ever-evolving. Universally defining sexuality is not possible, and what is deemed as "normal" is dependent on societal and cultural norms. As attitudes towards sexuality continue to progress, the definition of what is considered "normal" is constantly evolving. The existence of sex itself dates back to the beginning of time, as without it, life could not exist.

However, the first evidence of human opinions and beliefs about sex can be traced to ancient Hindu and Buddhist texts, which approached the topic from a moral and personal responsibility perspective (Jayatunge, 2014).

Human sexuality encompasses diverse facets, spanning from sexual orientation, denoting the preferred gender for attraction, to engagement in intimate acts like intercourse, kissing, and other forms of physical intimacy. It stands as one of the fundamental human drives, alongside the primal instincts of eating, fighting, and fleeing (Malacane & Beckmeyer, 2016), constituting a crucial aspect of the human condition and lived experience. Despite its significance, sexuality remains shrouded in societal taboos, resulting in a paucity of research compared to other primal instincts. This prompts introspection into the lingering stigma and reticence surrounding discussions on sexuality, urging an exploration of the underlying causes of shame and inhibition in this realm.

Throughout history, religious texts have played a pivotal role in shaping societal perceptions of sexuality, often imbuing it with moralistic undertones that fostered taboos and shame. Messages proliferated by these texts, portraying sex as inherently sinful or immoral and ostracizing individuals based on their sexual orientation or gender identity, have significantly contributed to the stigmatization of sexuality worldwide. Consequently, these narratives have hindered a comprehensive understanding of human sexuality. If sexuality were accorded the same level of scholarly scrutiny as other fundamental human behaviors like eating and sleeping, it could unveil valuable insights. Notably, pioneering researchers like Henry Havelock Ellis, who delved into the psychology of sex, emerged as proponents of gender and LGBTQ+

rights following their extensive studies. Ellis's seminal work, "Studies in the Psychology of Sex," not only advanced our understanding of human sexuality but also catalyzed advocacy efforts for marginalized communities.

This chapter delves into the sensitive topics of mistreatment, degradation, and misrepresentation of women. Many of the stories from ancient cultures provide misleading and harmful messages regarding women's sexuality, which is concerning. Unfortunately, the perspectives of women from these times have not been preserved, making it difficult to gain a true understanding of their lives (Roy, 2012). Additionally, women are often portrayed as obstacles to the spiritual path of male characters, further emphasizing our limited understanding of their experiences (Appleton, 2009). It is important to recognize these issues and work towards promoting a more equal and accurate representation of women in all aspects of life. As women make up more than half of the global population, understanding their experiences can provide invaluable insights for all individuals. Unfortunately, many societies still place the weight of patriarchy on women, leading to their marginalization in areas such as education, employment, and rights. This has hindered the advancement of gender equality. Sadly, women are often viewed as the "weaker sex," resulting in negative treatment and perceptions within society.

The narratives will be grouped into two overarching themes. The first category includes stories that depict women as inherently wicked without offering any justification for this portrayal. The second category involves stories where the husband abandons his wife, leaving her in the care of another man or entirely alone. Finally, we will examine three stories that do not fit neatly into either of these themes.

The Implication of Women's Wickedness in Jataka Stories

Notably, all the stories in this section seem to imply that women are inherently wicked. To delve deeper into these narratives, it is important to understand the underlying reasons for such implications and explore possible interpretations if this assumption is absent.

In the Asatamanta-jataka (Ja 61), a Brahmin family, concerned about the potential dangers posed by women, carefully raised their son. After completing his education under the respected teacher Bodhisatta, the son's mother convinced him he had not fully mastered the Dolour Texts, prompting him to return to his teacher.

Meanwhile, the Bodhisatta was devotedly caring for his elderly mother, meeting all her needs. Upon the student's return, he mentioned the Dolour Texts, which the teacher identified as a fabrication by the student's mother to impart her gender biases. The teacher then instructed the student to continue caring for his mother, highlighting her grace and beauty during her bathing routine. However, the mother misinterpreted her son's actions, believing he harbored romantic feelings for her, and even suggested killing the Bodhisatta to pursue their relationship. The story seems to suggest that some women possess undesirable qualities that attract young men, while also reflecting a prevalent misogyny and objectification in these types of narratives (Roy, 2012). Although the boy's actions may have contributed to the current situation, the unknown motivations and thoughts of the woman are ultimately considered "evil".

During this sequence, the student and Bodhisatta decide to test the mother's character after learning of her intentions. They create a wooden figure that resembles the Bodhisatta. The student asks the mother to strike it with an axe, believing it to be the sleeping Bodhisatta. The mother, who is blind, ends up striking the figure's throat, mistakenly believing she has killed her son. When confronted by the Bodhisatta, she is overcome with shock and passes away. The Bodhisatta then reveals to the student the true purpose of the Dolour Texts – to teach the student about the deceptive nature of women.

After returning home, the student shares with his mother that he has renounced family life and learned about the dangers of women's wickedness. He chooses to live as a hermit and remain chaste. The story implies that women's lust burns like a fire, yet it remains unclear why their desires are demonized when the student was the one who engaged in an affair. Despite the moral being conveyed, the story is still steeped in anti-woman language.

According to scholarly analysis, it has been determined that numerous stories exhibit a strong misogynistic tone (Appleton, 2009). This negativity towards women may have been intentional and crucial in maintaining the celibacy of Buddhist monks (Jones, 2001). For instance, this particular narrative where the female character serves as a form of temptation. The protagonist's ability to resist her allure signifies his dedication to a life of spiritual fulfillment and morality. It is apparent from the stories that celibacy is highlighted as a means to attain enlightenment, and women are often portrayed as seductresses who can steer men away from the spiritual path (Tanaka, 2006). As a result, the bias against women in these tales is probably meant to emphasize the significance of celibacy and righteousness in the teachings of Buddhism.

The Andabhuta-jataka (Ja 62) narrates a morally dubious action undertaken by the king's chaplain. In this tale, the chaplain embarks on a quest to find a woman who has not only abstained from sexual relations with other men but has also never laid eyes on any man. To achieve this, he adopts the strategy of raising a newborn baby girl within the confines of his household, closely monitored to prevent any interaction with men. To facilitate this endeavor, he compensates a destitute pregnant woman to reside within his premises until the birth of her baby girl, after which she is promptly dismissed with a token of gratitude.

Throughout her life, she was only cared for by women, except for the chaplain. One day, during a game, the king, who had been a Bodhisatta in a past life, lost to the chaplain. The Bodhisatta grew suspicious of a girl who was locked up in the chaplain's home and sought the help of a clever scamp to seduce her. The scamp opened a perfumery shop near the chaplain's store, and eventually, the mistress of the girl came to purchase items. Recognizing her as the mistress of the girl he was trying to win over, he introduced himself as her long-lost son who had been away for some time and respectfully bowed to her.

The onlookers witnessed a stir and recognized the resemblance between the lady and the young lad. Tears welled up in her eyes as she thought he might be her son. He inquired about her place of residence, to which she responded that she worked as a maid for the lovely lady at the chaplain's abode. The chaplain not only gifted her many fragrances and blooms but also provided complimentary items from his store, which brought them both immense joy. Subsequently, the woman kept the money given by the chaplain and procured all her flowers for free from the mischievous boy's shop.

As time passes, the mischievous boy feigns illness and expresses his love for the girl his mother admires. He insists that his love for her is so strong that he will perish if he cannot win her heart. His worried mother assures him that everything will be alright and presents the girl with a lovely collection of flowers and perfumes. She explains that her son has fallen for her and hopes that the girl feels the same way. Surprisingly, the girl expresses a desire to bring the boy into their home, which would relieve her of her work.

The mother sneaks her son into a house using a container of flower dust, and the girl and boy engage in a physical relationship. The story characterizes this act as "ruining the girl's reputation," reflecting outdated attitudes towards sexuality. In turn, they devise a plan to harm the chaplain in order to escape and be together. The mother blindfolds the chaplain and requests that he play the flute for her, pretending to be too shy to dance if he is watching. The young man emerges from hiding and strikes the chaplain, who is still blindfolded, on the head. Once the young man is safely out of harm's way, he informs the Bodhisatta of his success and what he has learned.

In the subsequent narrative development, the Bodhisatta opts to engage the chaplain in yet another game, resulting in the chaplain's defeat. Subsequent to this outcome, the Bodhisatta proceeds to disclose pertinent information to the chaplain, elucidating that the girl in question has forfeited her virtue. Despite enduring seclusion for the majority of her existence, she exhibits a reluctance to commit exclusively to the chaplain. Notably, an intriguing facet of the revelation is the attribution of fault to the girl, despite her having been subjected to circumstances beyond her control, having been abducted from birth, and denied a conventional existence due to the chaplain's insatiable sexual desires and lustful inclinations.

The narrative of this story serves as an elucidation of the perceived malevolence attributed to women. Explicitly, the tale directly addresses the reader, affirming this characterization towards its conclusion. The text articulates the notion that women are predisposed to resorting to any means, including criminal acts, to deceive their spouses, fundamentally underscoring their deceitful nature. Paralleling the antecedent narrative, the conspicuous omission of condemnation directed towards the male protagonist, who manipulates human life for personal gain, warrants scrutiny. Adopting a Western standpoint, it proves challenging to fathom a societal framework wherein the enslavement of a female from infancy, coupled with the deprivation of familial bonds, is condoned, let alone incites indignation when attempts at liberation are made.

Scholars have examined the misogynistic perspective presented in this story. It seems to depict a conflict of morals, as gambling is typically deemed immoral in Buddhist teachings, yet both the king and Bodhisatta are gamblers. Appleton (2009) points out that the questionable morality of the Bodhisatta paying someone to seduce a woman to maintain his winning streak is disregarded in favor of the message that one should be cautious of women, as even if you keep her by your side constantly, you cannot be certain of her (pp. 106). This may be attributed to the fact that these tales do not necessarily stem from Buddhist doctrine but rather from Indian Brahmanical literature, which is known for its misogyny (Bollee, 1970). In some classic texts, such as the Mahabharata and the Pali Canon, female characters are often depicted as dangerous, manipulative, or subservient to male characters. For instance, the Kosiya-jataka (Ja 130) recounts the story of a Brahmin student who is prevented from attending his teacher's lessons by his allegedly ill wife. The teacher, who is revealed to be a Bodhisatta, devises a scheme to help the student. However, his inner dialogue refers to the woman as a "creature," which clearly dehumanizes and belittles her. This is a clear example of misogyny in ancient literature.

The Bodhisatta asked the Brahmin to collect cow urine and some fruits, and to pickle the fruit in the cow urine in a copper pot so that both flavors would taste metallic. Following the Bodhisatta's recommendation, the Brahmin informs his wife that he will no longer provide her with delicacies and that she must swallow this "cure" for her illness, or she will have to begin earning her livelihood. In addition, at the Bodhisatta's suggestion, the Brahmin informs the wife that if she does not eat the disgusting mixture, he will drag her around by her hair and punch her. He claims that the mere threat of this should discourage the woman from refusing.

As expected, the woman refuses to eat the mixture, and the Brahmin tells her she will have to work for her food. He gives her an ultimatum: she can either remain sick (by refusing to consume the "cure") or eat. Eventually, the woman succumbs to fear and begins to do some housework. The story ends with the men (the Bodhisatta and Brahmin) being praised for being so conscious and converting the woman.

This particular story stands out due to its graphic portrayal of violence towards a woman, both physically and psychologically. However, the overarching theme emphasizes the importance of non-violence and prioritizes it over any negative moral depiction of women. Scholars have noted that these stories seem to reflect the beliefs and perspectives of the male authors and disseminators, rather than serving as accurate representations of Buddhist principles (Tambiah, 1992).

The Seggu-jataka (Ja 217) is a concise story in which the Bodhisatta appears as a tree spirit in a past life. A greengrocer tests his daughter by leading her into the forest and then pretends to be passionate with her by grabbing her hand. She refuses his advances, and he tells her that he is relieved she is pure and should not cry. She responds by saying that she does not commit such sins with men and wants to find a man who will keep her safe and company. The woman is afraid of her father due to his violent behavior. The greengrocer then gives his daughter in marriage back to his home after this ordeal.

Similar to the previous tale, the moral lesson of women's supposed wickedness is given more significance than the value of non-violence. The father assumes that his daughter will be "wicked" (with wickedness being equated to sexual activity), leading to the question of whether women can ever attain Buddhahood. This topic will be explored further in another story, but it is worth the reader's reflection at this point. These stories ostensibly depict the Bodhisatta's pursuit of Buddhahood, but what does it say about them if the foundation of Buddhist understanding is that women cannot achieve this state? Additionally, Appelton (2009) suggests that the jataka tales have contributed to the wide-spread belief that women are inferior to men and that the idea of women being unable to attain Buddhahood may be at the core of this belief.

According to the Kanavera-jataka (Ja 318), the Bodhisatta was depicted as a skilled and powerful thief in his past life. He was widely known for his elusive nature and his ability to evade capture. During one of his robberies at a wealthy merchant's house, he was caught by the king's order, subjected to brutal physical assault, executed, and ultimately met his death.

In a certain kingdom, there was a courtesan named Sama who offered her services at a cost of 1000 units of currency. She held a high standing with the king and was his favorite among the 500 enslaved women. Sama's heart was captured by the Bodhisatta's charm when she witnessed him being led to his death. In an effort to save his life, the queen came up with a plan and instructed a handmaid to offer the king 1000 coins, stating that the robber was her brother and that no one else could help. Unfortunately, the king remained dissatisfied and demanded that another man be executed in place of the robber.

As she eagerly anticipated the arrival of her daily visitor, who always brought her a generous gift of one thousand coins, her thoughts drifted to a painful secret she had been keeping hidden. Tears welled up in her eyes as he approached, and he immediately expressed concern for her welfare. Eventually, she summoned the courage to confide in him that her own brother was the thief who had stolen from the king, leaving her unable to provide the requested funds. Touched by his deep affection for her, he offered to assist and promptly delivered the money to the king. Regrettably, his act of kindness went unrecognized, resulting in his imprisonment while the Bodhisatta was surrendered to Sama. Regrettably, the young man was secretly executed, and the public remained unaware that he was not the notorious thief they had been led to believe he was.

The Bodhisatta and Sama enjoyed a blissful life together, deeply devoted to one another both emotionally and physically. However, the Bodhisatta's concern for the possibility of Sama's potential change of heart drove him to devise a protective plan. During a planned garden picnic, he embraced her so tightly that she lost consciousness, then departed with all of her jewelry.

After awakening, she asked her friends about the location of the Bodhisatta, but they had no answers. She assumed that he had found her motionless body among the plants and left, unaware that she had survived. This led her to sink into profound despair, neglecting her appearance, eating only one meal a day, and refraining from using the lavish items she had once loved. She went to great lengths, offering a reward of 1000 coins to send messengers to find the Bodhisatta. The messengers had to inform the Bodhisatta that Sama was still alive, as he had left believing she was dead. When they conveyed the news of her survival, they tracked down the Bodhisatta, but he doubted their message. Despite their descriptions of Sama's longing for him and assuring her loyalty, the Bodhisatta was unwavering in his decision to keep her at a distance. He feared that her presence would only cause pain. Sama was devastated by the Bodhisatta's response and ultimately went back to her previous occupation as a prostitute.

The piece under discussion delves into the intricacies of longing, exploring everything from fleeting infatuation to heartfelt love. One striking element is the female lead's successful career and recognition in her realm, which is closely linked to her profession in the realm of intimacy and the many suitors vying for her attention. Despite cultural norms that often favor men, women are still highly esteemed and celebrated. Regrettably, the story's unfavorable portrayal of women was intended to deter Buddhist monks from engaging in sexual relations (Jones, 2001), perpetuating a longstanding tradition of objectifying women in Asian societies. This works to further elevate men's status while diminishing female sexuality, thereby reinforcing the sacredness of monastic life.

The Kakati-jataka (Ja 327) recounts the tale of a prince who ascended to the throne after his father's passing. He wedded his chief queen, Kakati, who was celebrated for her beauty. During his reign, a king from Garudas came to his kingdom, disguised as a commoner, and played dice games with him. This king fell in love with the Bodhisatta's spouse and took her away to his kingdom without the Bodhisatta's knowledge. Eventually, the Bodhisatta yearned for his wife and dispatched a musician to Garudas to locate her. The musician found her and conveyed that she was missed at home because of her charm. The Garuda king acknowledged his mistake and returned her to the Bodhisatta.

This tale not only contradicts the principles of Buddhism regarding gambling but also sheds light on the problem of women being treated as possessions (Appleton, 2009). The queen, who remains unnamed throughout the story, has no say in her destiny and is subject to the whims of the men in her life. It is unclear why she is required to comply with not only her husband's wishes but also those of strangers she has not committed to. For instance, it is not clarified why she accompanied the new king to his kingdom. The narrative lacks insight into her own thoughts and motives, making it challenging to discuss her perspective. We are not even given her stance on being taken away by another king. These accounts emphasize the necessity of a more comprehensive female viewpoint in storytelling.

The Kharaputta-jataka (Ja 386) tells the story of Bodhisatta's past life as Sakka, where he was friends with Senaka, the king of Benares. Senaka had a close relationship with the naga king and was given a naga girl to care for and keep safe. If the girl ever went missing, the king would recite a charm to find her. One day, while the king was distracted by the lotuses in the garden, the naga girl transformed into a water snake to mate with another snake. When the king recited the charm to locate her, he found out about her actions and punished her with a bamboo strike.

In a fit of rage, she journeyed to the land of the nagas and accused Senaka of hitting her for not obeying his commands. The naga king, in response, commanded his young subjects to slay Senaka in his private quarters. As the young ones were nearing the end of their task, they happened to overhear Senaka inquiring of his spouse about the whereabouts of the naga maiden. Senaka proceeded to disclose that he had disciplined the naga girl by striking her with bamboo for indulging in misdeeds while in her serpent form. Upon being privy to this conversation, the young ones promptly made their way back to the naga ruler to convey the information they had gleaned.

Within the story, the king's experimentation with various charms and spells is delved into further. Ultimately, the tale culminates in a harrowing account of a woman enduring a vicious and severe beating, resulting in the loss of her skin. The reason for her punishment was an accusation of "greediness." It is noteworthy that similar actions taken by men are frequently deemed justifiable, courageous, or virtuous, while women are unfairly branded as selfish, foolish, or wicked. This story, among others in this collection, serves to illuminate the persistent conflict between Buddhist principles (including violence inflicted upon women's sexuality), society's inherent suspicion of women, and men's societal dominance.

The narrative of Sulasa-jataka (Ja 419) initially unfolds without explicit reference to matters of sexuality, yet as the story progresses, it emerges as a significant thematic element warranting consideration within the tale. As per the tale, there was a notorious robber by the name of Sattuka who wreaked havoc in the city. In response, the king ordered for the robber to be beheaded, so he could be caught and executed. In the same city resided a beautiful courtesan named Sulasa, who, upon witnessing the robber being taken away, instantly fell for him. She managed to free him by bribing the authorities, and the two of them lived together in a dignified manner for about three to four months. However, the robber grew restless and eventually decided to kill Sulasa and sell all her possessions.

After devising a plan, he informed Sulasa that he had made a commitment to a tree deity to offer something. He convinced her to join him and had them adorned in their finest jewelry and ornaments to present the offering. Upon reaching the mountain, he persuaded her to climb to the peak to avoid the throngs of people. However, she soon realized his true intentions of slaying her at the summit. Despite her affection towards him, she was shocked and repeatedly asked him why he would do such a thing. Quick-witted, she formulated a scheme to eliminate the attacker before he could kill her.

Through her clever ruse of performing blessings, Sulasa was able to outsmart and overpower the robber, ultimately sending him tumbling down the mountain to his demise. Witnessing her bravery, the tree deity appeared and commended her wise actions, noting that women are more than capable of such feats. Sulasa was widely celebrated for her quick thinking and ability to protect herself from harm. Interestingly, upon her return to the kingdom, she made no mention of her husband's tragic death.

This narrative presents a promising viewpoint on women. Buddhist literature does recognize the potential for women to achieve a significant spiritual awakening (known as Arahat), though it is important to note that this is viewed as distinct and less profound compared to attaining Buddha-hood, which is exclusively achievable for men (Appleton, 2009).

The Mahapaduma-jataka (Ja 472) recounts the tale of the Bodhisatta's past existence as a prince, whose father remarried after the death of his mother. One day, the stepmother is struck by the prince's striking appearance and proposes a sexual encounter in his father's absence. The Bodhisatta is taken aback and reminds her that she is his mother and also that she is married. Despite her insistence, he remains steadfast in his refusal. After three failed attempts to persuade him, she resorted to threatening him with the king's wrath. However, the situation took a turn for the worse when he finally relented. The queen found herself in a precarious position, unable to reveal her inappropriate advances toward her own son. Despite her coercive tactics, he steadfastly refused her advances, even when faced with the threat of execution.

When she approached the king, she made serious allegations against the Bodhisatta, claiming that he had made advances towards her and acted cruelly when she refused him. She urged the king to take action and have him put to death. Although the king was persuaded by her account and ordered the Bodhisatta to be arrested, restrained, and publicly shamed, the townspeople believed in his innocence and stood by him, demonstrating their unwavering support. When the Bodhisatta was brought before the king to face the charges, he adamantly refuted the woman's claims.

From this point on, the narrative shifts away from its primary focus on sexuality. Nevertheless, it maintains a central theme of deep-seated suspicion towards women, without any additional justification. While male characters in this segment engage in deceit and manipulation for personal gain, they are not saddled with the unjust stereotype that all men are inherently untrustworthy.

The Kunala-jataka (Ja 536) tells the story of Kanha, a young princess who falls in love with the five sons of Pandu. Despite the impossibility of marrying all five men, her parents allow it due to Kanha's intense passion. The men reciprocate her love, as does her disabled attendant. Kanha even tells him she would forsake the five other men and remain solely with him. Despite her declaration of preference for her eldest husband over his four brothers, it wasn't long before the brothers became suspicious of her behavior towards the disabled attendant. Certain telltale signs with her tongue revealed that they had been intimate before, causing the brothers to fall out of love with her and express their disgust at her choice of leaving them for a disabled man.

Although the brothers had no proof of the affair, the signs that the woman had been displaying were clear indicators that the two had been engaging in sexual activities. This, combined with the fact that she had chosen a disabled man over them, led to the brothers feeling betrayed and disgusted, which ultimately caused them to fall out of love with her. This suggests that this woman's behavior could be an example of someone who is struggling with a sexual addiction. The story continues to elaborate on other tales that have little to do with sexuality, so we won't discuss them in this section.

According to Appelton's analysis in 2009, this particular jataka story has been deemed highly misogynistic, as it suggests that women are predisposed to being avaricious and self-centered. While the summary provided may not fully convey why this story is considered as such, certain excerpts from the tale may serve to clarify this viewpoint. As an example, consider the following quote of the Kunala-jataka (Ja 536): "No man should trust women, for they are base, fickle, ungrateful and deceitful. They are ungrateful and do not act as they ought to; they do not care for their parents or brothers. Their actions are only motivated by their own desires, and they are mean and immoral. While men may be their loving, kind, and tender companions for a long time; though they may look to him as their own life, yet they often leave him in times of distress or misfortune. Therefore, I do not confide in women (Bollee, 1970)." This issue is complex, and it should be evident by now that this message is harmful and, in reality, inaccurate.

It's worth noting that the distrustfulness present in society seems to be directed primarily towards women, without any clear justification for this bias. It begs the question: what makes men exempt from being ungrateful or deceitful at times? Interestingly, a number of jataka stories, even those not mentioned in this chapter, portray men behaving in a manipulative, greedy, and deceitful manner. Why is it that when women act in such a way, it is often attributed to their inherent nature, while men are not held to the same standard? This double standard is difficult to overlook.

There seems to be a societal bias that devalues women and their worth compared to men, highlighted by the emphasis placed on caring for "parents or brothers." While it's reasonable to assume that mothers are included in the definition of "parents," what about sisters? Shouldn't it be equally admirable to care for one's sister? Additionally, when describing marriage or partnership, it's typically the man who is characterized as the "loving, kind, and tender companion." The question arises as to why the woman's role in the context of intimate relationships remains marginalized and unrecognized. Additionally, the assumption prevailing in societal constructs that the husband inherently embodies qualities of love and affection by default warrants scrutiny. Empirical investigations, exemplified by Johnson (2005), have consistently evidenced a predominant male involvement in instances of domestic violence. Furthermore, scholarly inquiries such as those conducted by Holtzworth-

Munroe et al. (2000) reveal a correlation between perpetration of domestic violence and harboring misogynistic attitudes among male perpetrators. Consequently, the propagation of misogynistic ideologies, akin to those depicted within the section of Jataka stories under examination, could potentially exacerbate the likelihood of occurrences of intimate partner violence.

Husband Leaving Home

In addition to the previously mentioned misogynistic messages present in these stories, a specific theme persists throughout. The husbands frequently leave their homes for extended periods, leaving another man in charge of their wife. This is where the conflicts typically arise. Many of these tales insinuate that a woman requires a man to look after her in her husband's absence, yet simultaneously suggest that she is untrustworthy and will betray her spouse as soon as he departs. The conspicuous absence of any explanation as to why a wife would betray her controlling husband in certain narratives raises questions about the underlying assumptions and perspectives of those stories. It appears that the perspective of the female character is often overlooked or undervalued in such instances.

The Mudulakkhana-jataka (Ja 66) tells the story of a Bodhisatta born into a wealthy Brahmin family who later renounced all worldly desires and lived a secluded life in the Himalayas. During this time, he attained higher levels of knowledge and led a serene and mystical existence. One day, while in need of salt and vinegar, he took up residence in the king's garden. As he was leaving the palace with his belongings slung over his shoulder to request alms in the kingdom, the king saw him at the gate and was so impressed that he invited the Bodhisatta to stay permanently in the garden. For 16 years, he lived with the king and savored the finest food and drink.

After some time, the king departed from the palace to tend to his royal duties. Before leaving, he entrusted his wife, the queen, with the task of catering to the needs of the Bodhisatta. During the king's absence, the queen diligently attended to the Bodhisatta's needs, providing him with food and other necessities. On one occasion, the Bodhisatta arrived later than usual, and the queen took advantage of the time to bathe in perfumed water. As she eagerly awaited the Bodhisatta's arrival, she heard him approaching and quickly rose to meet him. In her haste, her robe slipped off, leaving her completely naked.

Upon witnessing her undressed form, all lessons of insight and morality were rendered powerless in his mind as pure pleasure took over. His desire for her was all-consuming. After partaking in the meal she had prepared, he found himself overwhelmed with longing and retreated to the garden where he remained motionless for a full week, without sustenance. His infatuation with the queen had consumed him entirely. On the seventh day, the King returned to find the Bodhisatta in his garden cell, and inquired anxiously as to what troubled him. The Bodhisatta confessed that he was ill with an insatiable lust for the queen. In a troubling example of women being treated as objects, the king promised to give the queen to the Bodhisatta if he desired her deeply enough. As they left the kingdom together, the king instructed someone to take care of the Bodhisatta, though it's unclear whether the queen was aware of this. Along the way, the queen suggested they ask the king for a house, but the one they were given was filthy and unacceptable to her. The Bodhisatta cleaned the house and even plastered the walls with cow dung, after obtaining the necessary supplies from the king. Afterwards, the queen instructed the Bodhisatta to obtain a bed, stool, rug, water pot, and cup, insisting that he make separate trips for each item. Once this was accomplished, she gazed into the Bodhisatta's eyes and reminded him of his sacred status. It was then that the Bodhisatta regained his composure, recollecting all of his teachings on wisdom and ethics. As a result, he resolved to bring the queen back to the king and depart for the mountains.

The lesson conveyed in this narrative pertains solely to women in their role as wives. It implies that wives are often bothersome and entitled, lacking the willingness to put in the effort to achieve their desires. Interestingly, the wife in the story actually subscribes to this notion, indicating that misogyny has become ingrained within her. Studies have shown that internalized misogyny can intensify the emotional impact of a sexist encounter on a woman (Szymanski et al., 2009). Additionally, the more a woman is conditioned to believe that she is inferior and less significant than men, the more she may experience distress when treated as mere property. Considering the narrative in its entirety, it appears apparent that the queen and king have maintained a long-standing culture of misogyny, in which the female party does not challenge the behaviors that diminish her worth as an individual. As a consequence, we observe the queen being deprived of her title and being forced to vacate the palace without being given a chance to demonstrate her innocence. This serves as a stark illustration of the power differential between the two individuals and its adverse effects on the queen's mental and emotional state.

According to the Bandhanamokkha-jataka (Ja 120), Bodhisatta was born into a chaplain's family and eventually became a chaplain himself following his father's passing. During this time, the king made a promise to his queen that he would fulfill any request she had. In response, she asked him to refrain from looking at other women in a lustful or loving way. Although he initially refused, the king eventually gave in and never again gazed lovingly upon the 16,000 girls who danced for his entertainment.

Once, the king was called away on royal duties that involved violence, and the queen was not permitted to accompany him. To alleviate her worries, the king sent a messenger every hour to assure her of his safety, and vice versa. Shockingly, the queen slept with every one of the 230 messengers the King sent to her. As the king returned to the kingdom, he continued to send messengers every hour to update the queen on their progress, and again, she slept with each and every one of them.

As the Bodhisatta was preparing for the king's return, he noticed the queen's attraction towards him. She attempted to seduce him into sleeping with her, but the Bodhisatta firmly declined. The queen taunted him, claiming that other messengers had taken her up on her offer. The Bodhisatta assured her that he was an individual with unique values and would not be swayed like the others. In response, the queen threatened him with death if he did not comply. Undeterred, the Bodhisatta replied that he would rather lose his head than commit such a sin. As a result, the queen feigned illness and retired to bed in a fit of rage.

Sexuality: Exploring Human Relationships and Identity

Upon witnessing the queen's distressed state, the king inquired about the cause. The queen explained that she had been beaten by the Bodhisatta, as she had refused to engage in intimate activities with him. Infuriated by this news, the king ordered the Bodhisatta's capture, binding, and execution. Upon being apprehended, the Bodhisatta suspected that the queen had manipulated the king into turning against him. As a result, he devised a plan to speak with the king before his execution, citing the potential loss of the king's treasures if he were to perish.

In a display of eloquence, the Bodhisatta presents the situation to the king upon being brought before him. When the queen confesses to having slept with all the messengers, the king orders their execution. However, the Bodhisatta intervenes and argues that the men are innocent and that the queen should be held accountable instead. The Bodhisatta goes on to explain that the queen's behavior is not entirely her fault, as it is influenced by her inherent nature as a woman. The king is touched by the Bodhisatta's words and decides to show mercy by sparing all lives and providing them with homes.

The Radha-jataka (Ja 198) tells of a Brahmin who treats his two parrots, Radha (the Bodhisatta) and Potthapada, like his own children. However, the introduction of the Brahmin's wife as wicked perpetuates the negative portrayal of women seen in these tales. The story also features the husband entrusting the parrots to watch over his wife while he is away on business, implying that women are incapable of controlling their impulses. The wife's subsequent behavior, while not explicitly stated as wrong, is likely to involve male visitors. This double standard reinforces harmful gender roles and contributes to gender inequality.

Psychological Aspects of Jataka Stories

Seeing this, the parrots became angry with her, and Potthapada inquired as to why she was committing so many sins. As she was angry and wanted to kill him, she pretended to hug him. When they embraced, she yelled at him in anger, wrung his neck, and threw him into the oven. When the husband returned, he asked Radha about what had happened while he was gone.

Here, the story becomes a little cryptic. According to him, his brother spoke of things that were not conducive to blessings (probably scolding his mother) and as a result, he was burned and later died. Also, he stated that he could not tell him the truth because Potthapada revealed the truth and died as a result. Additionally, he realized that he did not wish to live with them anymore, so Radha bid the Brahmins farewell and flew off into the forest.

The question arises as to what constitutes a lie: is it the purposeful telling of untruths, or does it also encompass omitting to tell true ones? In this instance, lying is considered a more acceptable feat than telling the truth about his mother and risking death. The story does not elaborate further on this so it is difficult to unravel the rationale behind this, but it is a notable deviation from the other stories in this chapter.

The Harita-jataka (Ja 431) depicts the Bodhisatta as a learned member of a Brahmin family called Harittaca-kumara in his previous life. As an adult, he became a holy man, and one day, he ventured into the city seeking alms and other provisions. The king, upon seeing him, graciously invited him to the palace to partake in a royal feast. Eventually, the Bodhisatta was provided with lodgings by the king for a period of twelve years. On one occasion, the king had to leave town for business and entrusted the care of the queen to the Bodhisatta. On a particular evening, after bathing in fragrant water, the queen appeared quite beautiful. When the Bodhisatta returned, she hurriedly rose from her seat, causing her garments to slip off (a situation similar to the Mudu-lakkhana-jataka). Upon seeing her unclothed form, the Bodhisatta succumbed to desire, momentarily forgetting his principles. He took hold of her hand, and the two engaged in intimacy. Afterwards, he had a light refreshment and retired to his quarters in the park.

The ascetic's misconduct persisted for several days until the townspeople discovered it and wrote a letter to the king, informing him of the situation. However, the king was initially skeptical and asked the queen for confirmation, but even her word wasn't enough to convince him. Seeking the truth, the king turned to the wise Bodhisatta for guidance. Though the Bodhisatta had committed a transgression by giving in to lust, he knew that honesty was an essential component of achieving enlightenment. Therefore, he revealed to the king that humans are vulnerable to four passions: lust, hate, excess, and ignorance.

The Bodhisatta's conduct differs markedly from that of the previous tale, where preserving life took precedence over telling the truth. The reason behind the sudden shift towards endorsing dishonesty remains unclear. Nonetheless, these discrepancies lend weight to the assertions put forth earlier in this chapter, suggesting that these stories may not necessarily conform to Buddhist principles and values, but rather reflect the viewpoints and customs of the Indian authors who authored and propagated them (Appleton, 2009).

Homosexuality

Although not overtly focused on homosexual themes, the ensuing stories portray deep and intimate connections between two men. Therefore, the concept of close male relationships is not necessarily unfamiliar or unnatural. However, it is important to note that these stories only depict male-male relationships and cannot be used to make any generalizations about homosexuality. Research suggests that there is no clear evidence on how the Buddha felt about homosexuality, other than the belief that as long as the relationship is founded on love and avoids causing harm, it is not immoral to engage in a romantic relationship with someone of the same gender. The following two stories only imply homosexuality as a theme.

The Mani-Kantha-jataka (Ja 253) is a heartwarming tale of friendship without any explicit sexual content. The story follows the Bodhisatta, who is born as the son of a wealthy Brahmin alongside his younger brother. After the death of their parents, they seek refuge in huts near the Ganges River. One day, a serpent king named Manikantha takes human form and befriends the younger brother. They spend time together every day and even exchange hugs before parting ways. Despite their pleasant friendship, the man begins to lose weight due to his fear of the serpent, which seems puzzling. Once upon a time, the Bodhisatta paid a visit to his ailing brother and was distressed to see his yellowed skin and bulging veins. The brother confided that a serpent was to blame and was advised by the Bodhisatta to request the serpent's precious jewel. This would put an end to the serpent's appearance and allow him to recover. Sure enough, the plan proved successful. However, the serpent grew weary of the man's persistent appeals for the jewel, as he was reluctant to part with it, and stopped showing up altogether. Unfortunately, the man's condition began to worsen once the serpent stopped appearing.

Upon inquiring about his well-being, the Bodhisatta learns that the man is unwell due to his inability to reunite with his dearest friend, the serpent king. The Bodhisatta cautions the man about the potential dangers of love and how it can lead one to plead in desperation. The tale also highlights how the act of begging caused the serpent king to lose interest in their friendship. Although the story contains some sensuous elements, its underlying message appears to emphasize the importance of true friendship. The depiction of the man and the serpent's bond is profound, vivid, and brimming with warmth.

According to the Kesava-jataka (Ja 346), the Bodhisatta's past life involved growing up in a Brahmin household as Kappa. He formed a close bond with another ascetic named Kesava, and they both embraced a spiritual existence. During their friendship, Kesava accompanied the other ascetics to Benares to procure salt and vinegar and was invited to the king's garden, where they were provided with food and accommodations.

In due course, Kesava expressed his desire to depart from the garden, but the king kindly offered him the option to stay, as he himself was in his advanced years and could send the younger ascetics back to the Himalayas. Kesava graciously accepted the invitation to remain in the king's garden, while his fellow ascetic, Kappa, journeyed to the Himalayas. Kesava's separation from his dear friend caused him great distress, leading to sleepless nights and difficulty eating. Sadly, he developed an internal ailment due to his inability to properly digest his food.

Upon being asked what would heal him, Kesava requested to return to the Himalayas to spend time with Kappa once again. The king agreed and sent foresters to accompany him. Upon reuniting with Kappa, Kesava was immediately cured of his illness and depression after drinking an unseasoned broth of millet and wild rice that Kappa had prepared.

Later on, the king sent a messenger to check on Kesava's well-being, who asked about Kappa's healing techniques since none of the royal treatments had worked. Kesava spoke highly of the Himalayas and Kappa's teachings, and explained how the unseasoned broth had cured him. When asked about asceticism, Kesava confirmed that it was indeed a way of life for them. He concluded with a heartwarming message that a meal prepared with love has the power to cure all illnesses, regardless of its simplicity.

"Love is undoubtedly the most delectable seasoning one could ever taste." Among the heartwarming messages in this collection of stories, this one stands out. It focuses on the theme of love rather than sexuality, which is a refreshing change. Interestingly, there are no female characters in this particular story. This is not to suggest that the presence of women automatically implies sexual undertones, but it is intriguing to note that whenever a woman (or a wife or a queen) appears in the other stories, there is usually a sexual moral lesson to be learned. This observation indicates that women in literature are often associated with sexual messages, even when they are not directly related to the story's primary subject matter. This may reflect a certain attitude towards women in these stories.

Sexual Satisfaction

The Sattubhasta-jataka (Ja 402) contains a notable section that is tangentially connected to the themes of sexuality explored in this tale. The narrative commences with a Brahmin who is destitute and soliciting funds. As his financial resources dwindle, he is compelled to offer his daughter's hand in marriage to settle a debt. The young woman is wed to another Brahmin and relocates to a neighboring village. Unfortunately, her spouse fails to meet her physical needs, prompting her to engage in infidelity with a different individual. The narrative comes to a pause, and the focus shifts to the sixteen things in life that are insatiable. Among them, the king can never be content with his kingdom, the talker can never be satisfied with their words, and a woman can never be fulfilled with her sexual encounters. The depiction of a woman's unfulfilled sexual desires in her marriage is emblematic of the overall dissatisfaction one can experience in life. This tale serves as a poignant reminder that, regardless of one's acquisitions, there will always be an element that remains unfulfilled.

This is the point at which one should take a moment to reflect. The list of things that cannot be satisfied is quite extensive, spanning from the metaphorical and abstract (such as a sea not being satisfied by rivers) to the literal and concrete (such as women frequently feeling unsatisfied with sex). It's remarkable that this is considered a fundamental truth of reality rather than a sign of the general experience women have with men. In other words, men tend to blame a woman's lack of sexual satisfaction on something inherently wrong with her, rather than considering the possibility that they may not be skilled lovers. Research has actually shown that many women experience sexual dissatisfaction (Shah Hosseini et al., 2014). It is important to note that dissatisfaction in the bedroom cannot always be attributed to a woman's marital status. In fact, it appears to transcend these distinctions. One possible explanation for this phenomenon could be that men sometimes lack the necessary understanding and empathy to fulfill women's needs. Instead, they may rely on outdated stereotypes and assumptions, which can unfairly place blame on their partners. This dynamic can leave women feeling unheard and unappreciated, ultimately leading to a lack of sexual satisfaction.

The perception of sex among men often diverges from viewing it as a cooperative and intimate act, instead regarding women primarily as conduits for their own gratification. Consequently, if this perspective prevails, women's sexual fulfillment becomes contingent upon unlikely circumstances. Moreover, from an evolutionary standpoint, women are inherently disadvantaged as their reproductive process does not necessitate sexual pleasure, unlike men, who must achieve climax to produce semen. This biological reality, however, fails to encapsulate the broader spiritual, emotional, and psychological dimensions integral to a fulfilling and connected sexual experience. In the historical context of male treatment towards women, the latter have been perceived not as sexual beings but rather as entities solely responsible for perpetuating the human species. As a consequence, women's sexual satisfaction has not been afforded prioritization.

Conclusion

The Jataka stories collectively present a nuanced yet discernible portrayal of how their compilers intended readers to perceive women and sexuality. These narratives underscore the significance attributed to abstaining from sexual activity, often achieved through the denigration of women. They thus serve as reflective artifacts of the authors' values, notably advocating for female chastity until marriage. This notion is further reinforced through insinuations that women who engage in premarital intercourse are cast as promiscuous, morally deficient, and socially inferior individuals. As Appleton (2009) posits, the Jataka stories have transcended mere folklore, acquiring a heightened significance due to their association with the Buddha's narrative as a Bodhisatta. Despite scholarly temptations to regard these Jataka tales as products of a multifaceted historical evolution rather than as authoritative sources of Buddhist doctrine, their enduring influence on societal attitudes and behaviors in South and Southeast Asia cannot be understated. Thus, a comprehensive study of the Jataka stories is warranted to elucidate the underlying values and beliefs embedded within Buddhist culture. Furthermore, while serving as valuable resources for Buddhist practitioners and scholars, these stories have also been criticized for reinforcing gender roles and stereotypes, potentially perpetuating gender inequality and power differentials within these regions.

References

Appleton, N. (2009). Temptress on the path: Women as objects and subjects in Buddhist jataka stories. In *New topics in feminist philosophy of religion* (pp. 103-115). Springer, Dordrecht.

Holtzworth-Munroe, A., Meehan, J. C., Herron, K., Rehman, U., & Stuart, G. L. (2000). Testing the Holtzworth-Munroe and Stuart (1994) batterer typology. *Journal of Consulting and Clinical Psychology*, 68(6), 1000-1019. https://doi.org/10.1037/0022-006X.68.6.1000

Human Rights Campaign Foundation. (n.d.). *Stances of faiths on LGBTQ issues: Buddhism*. https://www.hrc.org/resources/stances-of-faiths-on-lgbt-issues-buddhism

Jayatunge, R. M. (2014, October 11). *Human sexuality discussed in the Jataka stories*. LankaWeb. https://www.lankaweb.com/news/items/2014/10/11/human-sexuality-discussed-in-the-jataka-stories/

Johnson, M. P. (2005). Domestic violence: It's not about gender: Or is it? *Journal of Marriage and the Family*, 67(5), 1126-1130. https://doi.org/10.1111/j.1741-3737.2005.00206.x

Jones, J. G. (2001). *Tales and teachings of the Buddha*: The Jataka stories in relation to the Pali Canon.

Kabilsingh, C. (1991). *Thai women in Buddhism*. Parallax Press.

Malacane, M., & Beckmeyer, J. J. (2016). A review of parent-based barriers to parent–adolescent communication about sex and sexuality: Implications for sex and family educators. *American Journal of Sexuality Education*, 11(1), 27-40. https://doi.org/10.1080/15546128.2016.1146187

Roy, T. (2012). The notion of objectifying women: As represented in the Jatakas. *Proceedings of the Indian History Congress*, 73, 126–131.

Shahhosseini, Z., Gardeshi, Z. H., Pourasghar, M., & Salehi, F. (2014). A review of affecting factors on sexual satisfaction in women. *Materia Sociomedica*, 26(6), 378–381. https://doi.org/10.5455/msm.2014.26.378-381

Szymanski, D. M., Gupta, A., Carr, E. R., & Stewart, D. (2009). Internalized misogyny as a moderator of the link between sexist events and women's psychological distress. *Sex Roles*, 61(1-2), 101-109. https://doi.org/10.1007/s11199-009-9611-y

Tambiah, S. J. (1992). *Buddhism betrayed?: Religion, politics, and violence in Sri Lanka*. University of Chicago Press.

CHAPTER SIX

SUBSTANCE ABUSE: COPING MECHANISMS AND MORAL LESSONS IN JATAKA STORIES

Introduction

The issue of substance abuse is a growing concern that affects individuals worldwide, regardless of their age, race, or socioeconomic status. Substance abuse can lead to severe physical, psychological, and social consequences. Although the dangers of alcohol consumption have been recognized for centuries, people continue to consume it. According to the World Health Organization, approximately 283 million individuals worldwide suffer from alcohol use disorders (WHO, 2018), and this number continues to rise.

Substance Abuse: Coping Mechanisms and Moral Lessons

According to the latest report by the World Health Organization, alcohol consumption is responsible for approximately 3 million deaths globally each year, which makes up 5.3% of all deaths. Moreover, harmful alcohol use contributes to 5.1% of the global burden of disease and injuries, and leads to a 7.2% burden of disease and injuries among males. Those aged 20-49 are particularly at risk, with alcohol accounting for 25% of all deaths in this age group (WHO, 2018). It is important to note that disadvantaged and vulnerable populations are often disproportionately affected by alcohol - related death and hospitalization in most countries.

Addiction to substances, as delineated by Singh (2020), encompasses an array of characteristics, including an insatiable compulsion for drug intake, escalating dosage patterns, psychological and physical reliance, and detrimental impacts on personal and social spheres. These criteria are aptly applied in the discourse surrounding alcohol abuse disorders, which often manifest in uncontrollable drinking patterns, frequent binge episodes, and an incapacity to curtail alcohol consumption despite adverse repercussions. The addictive nature of alcohol lies in its ability to hijack the brain's reward circuitry, prioritizing alcohol consumption over fundamental physiological needs such as food, rest, and intimacy (Volkow et al., 2016), consequently fostering the development of alcoholism—a chronic and potentially fatal condition if left untreated. Concurrently, alcohol abuse engenders a spectrum of health complications, spanning from liver and cardiovascular ailments to malignancies and cerebrovascular events. In the realm of jataka narratives, alcohol serves as a catalyst for personal and societal downfall, often depicted through the initiation of novice drinkers and their subsequent entanglement in calamitous circumstances. Furthermore, alcohol consumption in these tales is frequently entwined with criminal behaviors such as theft or assault. The forthcoming discussion within this chapter will expound upon two overarching themes: the ramifications of alcohol addiction and the negative societal stigma attached to alcohol consumption, while also addressing the pivotal role of supportive figures in the journey toward recovery from alcoholism.

Consequences of Alcohol Addiction

Before delving into the topic of addiction, it is worth noting that alcohol consumption does not necessarily equate to harmful or problematic behavior. In fact, many people consume alcohol to alleviate pain, improve sleep, and relieve feelings of anxiety, depression, and stress (Ferguson et al., 2022). However, not all of these individuals exhibit signs of problematic or disordered alcohol dependence. This indicates that the quality and context of alcohol consumption, not just the quantity, are crucial factors to consider when assessing alcohol use disorder. To accurately evaluate such a disorder, it is important to take into account the individual's motivations, behaviors, and drinking patterns.

According to Eashwar et al. (2020), researchers have identified various patterns of alcohol consumption that may or may not be problematic or harmful. For instance, "social drinking" refers to consuming two drinks (for men) or one drink (for women) in a social setting and waiting several days before drinking again. This type of drinking is generally considered safe and not harmful. However, other patterns like "binge drinking," "harmful drinking," "hazardous drinking," and "alcohol dependence" typically require clinical intervention and can lead to severe physical and psychological consequences, including health problems, impaired functioning, and damaged personal relationships.

Alcohol addiction, or excessive alcohol consumption, can have severe physical and social consequences. However, it is essential to understand that consuming alcohol does not automatically indicate addiction. According to the Diagnostic and Statistical Manual of Mental Disorders (DSM-5; APA, 2013), Alcohol Use Disorder is characterized by the inability to control or stop drinking, even when negative consequences arise in different areas of life. Therefore, when diagnosing an alcohol-related disorder, it is crucial to consider the severity of its impact and its overall effect on the individual's life.

The World Health Organization's European Region has the highest alcohol consumption globally, contributing to premature mortality and various illnesses. Annually, alcohol-related fatalities in the region approach nearly 1 million, leading to unintentional and intentional injuries. Prenatal exposure to alcohol causes fetal alcohol spectrum disorders (FASD), which are entirely avoidable. Alcohol consumption also accounts for a quarter of deaths among individuals aged 20 to 24, negatively affecting demographic trends, economic growth, and productivity in the region (WHO, 2018).

Some Jataka stories portray the harmful effects of alcohol consumption, which can be compared to contemporary research on alcohol-related disorders. These stories serve as a potent reminder of the consequences of excessive drinking, emphasizing the need for responsible consumption of alcohol. By analyzing these tales in conjunction with current research, we can gain a better understanding of the risks associated with alcohol abuse and work towards building a healthier society.

The Kumbha-jataka (Ja 512) is a notable tale that delves into the topic of substance abuse. This narrative details the unearthing of alcohol and serves as a warning regarding the perils of substance misuse. The plot centers on a naturally occurring crevice in a tree's bark that accumulates rainwater. Adjacent fruit trees occasionally drop their produce into this crevice. This narrative is considered significant as it highlights the perils of substance abuse. Nearby, there was a rice paddy where parrots would pick at the rice, causing the husked grains to fall into a nearby water hole. The combination of these ingredients and the sun's heat resulted in the fermentation of the water, fruit, and rice, ultimately leading to the creation of alcohol. Various animals, such as birds, dogs, and monkeys, would consume the alcoholic beverage and become inebriated. A forester named Sura noticed this peculiar behavior and decided to examine the liquor. He discovered that although it was not poisonous, it had a unique effect on the animals who drank it. They would fall asleep for a few hours, only to wake up and continue their daily activities without any signs of a hangover or weakness.

He decided to try the liquor himself. He became drunk and suddenly had a craving for meat after doing so. This is an interesting note that appears in several of the stories where someone drinks alcohol for the first time. Several studies have shown that excessive alcohol consumption is associated with poorer diets, unsatisfactory weight control, body dissatisfaction, and sedentary behavior (Nelson et al., 2009). This indicates that alcohol consumption can lead to unhealthy dietary patterns and physical activity levels. It is also true that alcohol consumption is associated with decreased inhibitions (Lane et al., 2004), so it is natural to become ravenous for a delicacy that you normally abstain from after drinking alcohol. Consequently, he roasted several birds, ate them, and continued to eat and drink in this area for a couple of days.

Afterward, Sura recollected a hermit named Varuna, whom he occasionally visited, and decided to share some liquor with him. He brought along some meat, and both of them enjoyed a feast. They took the liquor to the king, who drank it and asked for more when his small stock depleted. The king kept requesting more liquor, so instead of going back to the Himalayas, Sura and Varuna gathered the ingredients to make the liquor in the city. The townsfolk adored it and drank it whenever they could. Consequently, they became lazy and neglected their duties, and the town became deserted. The same scenario repeated when Sura and Varuna brought the liquor to another city.

After traveling to Savatthi, Sura and Varuna produced five hundred jars of liquor. To protect the precious jars, they stationed cats to guard them. However, when the fermentation process caused the jars to overflow, the cats indulged in the liquor, became inebriated, and fell into a deep slumber. During their sleep, rats snuck in and nibbled on the cats' ears, noses, teeth, and tails. When the king's officials discovered the cats the next day, they assumed they had died from consuming the liquor. The king, therefore, inferred that the liquor was poisonous and ordered Sura and Varuna's execution while also commanding for the jars to be destroyed. But, upon inspection, the officers found that the cats were still alive. The king soon realized that it was only alcohol and drank it in the company of his courtiers.

When the king of heaven, Sakka, noticed the king of earth drinking liquor, he became worried that it would cause harm to the entire kingdom. To help, he assumed the form of a Brahmin and offered the king a jar of liquor, attempting to sell it to him. When the king inquired, Sakka warned him about the wicked qualities of liquor, including alcohol, fats, and sugar, which can corrupt one's virtuous nature. The king was informed of the risks of excessive drinking, which can lead to shameless behavior, physical tremors, and even death. Sakka referred to wine as a substance that shelters thieves and the ungodly. He advised that those who partake become filled with unwarranted pride and that alcohol can transform the most righteous man into a murderer and the most wise man into a fool. The king took Sakka's cautionary tale to heart and ceased drinking alcohol.

While the depiction of a city descending into ruin due to alcohol consumption may be a dramatization meant to convey a message through narrative, it remains accurate that alcohol use can have far-reaching negative consequences that go beyond the individual and their loved ones. In fact, Bonu et al. (2005) found a correlation between alcohol use and impoverishment. The impoverishment was caused by borrowing money and selling off assets in order to pay medical bills for the alcoholism. Researchers have found that people who are dependent on alcohol spend more than they earn and are forced to take out loans to cover their alcohol-related expenses (Benegal et al., 2000). The impact of financial insecurity can be far-reaching, affecting not just the individual but also their family and the wider society. It can result in a decline in overall quality of life and contribute to the rise of poverty and social inequality. The story at hand offers several poignant examples that exemplify the devastating effects of such insecurity.

The story of Illisa-jataka (Ja 78) highlights the damaging effects of alcohol addiction on society. Illisa, a central character in this tale, is portrayed as the Bodhisatta in the Varuni-jataka (Ja 47) and Punnapati-jataka (Ja 53). However, unlike his virtuous counterparts, Illisa's obsession with wealth leads him to hoard all the riches of the city. One day, he sees a traveler enjoying dried fish and a drink of alcohol and becomes enamored with the idea of imbibing himself. Despite his craving, Illisa refrains from drinking, knowing that others in the kingdom would follow suit and he would be responsible for providing them with alcohol at a cost. As time passes, he finds it increasingly difficult to resist his addiction, and his physical appearance deteriorates, displaying symptoms of severe liver disease like jaundice. This is a poignant reminder of the harmful consequences of excessive alcohol consumption.

Eventually, succumbing to his craving, he dispatched a servant to the tavern to fetch some liquor. To add to this, his wife offered to prepare a limited quantity of liquor for his exclusive consumption. Since then, he has been exclusively indulging in alcohol. His father, who led a virtuous life and was reborn as Sakka, observed his son's misguided decisions and resolved to make him comprehend the repercussions of his actions.

According to the story, Sakka took on the persona of Illisa in order to guide an individual towards virtuous behavior and earn a place in heaven. Disguised as Illisa, he approached the king and offered to distribute his wealth as he saw fit, which the king accepted. Upon returning to

Illisa's home in his true form, Sakka informed his family and servants of his plans to share his wealth. They were impressed by his newfound generosity, though they speculated that he may have imbibed something to inspire such behavior.

It is intriguing to note that indulging in alcohol has been associated with favorable results. Whether or not drinking should be deemed unethical if it results in courteous conduct is a contemplative matter, not within the purview of this piece. According to research conducted by Ferguson et al. (2022), alcohol consumption may aid individuals in managing stress and anxiety, potentially leading to an enhanced state of composure. Nevertheless, this may only be a temporary fix, as prolonged alcohol intake can adversely impact one's mental well-being.

When Illisa announced his decision to give away his wealth, the people of the city flocked to him in droves, eager to fill their vessels with as much riches as possible. Among them was a countryman who had worked for Illisa. The man took Illisa's oxen and carriage, filling them to the brim with treasure before departing. Overjoyed, he sang praises of Illisa all the way home, feeling incredibly grateful. It was not until he encountered the real Illisa down the road, still drinking alone, that he realized his mistake. Illisa overheard the man's praises and grew confused and frightened, unsure of why he was being lauded in such a way.

When Illisa discovered that someone was giving away his riches, he was stricken with panic and promptly made efforts to retrieve them. However, his endeavors to regain ownership of his oxen and carriage proved fruitless, as Sakka had taken on the guise of Illisa and instructed the townsfolk to disregard any individual resembling him as a fraud. This scheme was successful, as upon Illisa's return home, his servants refused him entry. In time, Sakka revealed his true identity, and Illisa vowed to maintain his generous ways.

In this narrative, Illisa develops an alcohol dependency, his sole focus becoming the consumption of alcohol. It is intriguing to consider that Illisa may have possessed inherent hedonistic inclinations that became fixated on alcohol upon discovery. Additionally, the presence of a genetic predisposition towards alcohol dependence is noteworthy. It is intriguing to speculate whether Illisa's father's apprehension regarding his son's behavior stems from recognizing similar traits in another family member, though this remains speculative as the story does not explicitly mention it.

Additionally, research shows that the sons of male alcoholics are more susceptible to alcohol use disorders (Pihl et al., 1990). In fact, studies indicate that these individuals are 50 to 60 percent more likely to develop alcohol use disorders compared to the general population (pubs.niaaa.nih.gov). They tend to display behavioral, cognitive, and psychological differences, such as disruptive behavior, hyperactivity, poor verbal and cognitive abilities, and academic struggles. It would be intriguing to investigate whether Illisa had similar experiences during her childhood. However, it is important to note that these genetic predispositions can occur even if the father is not an alcoholic. Although there is a link between offspring of alcoholic fathers and potential variances in behavior, cognition, and psychological traits, it is important to recognize that other factors may also influence these outcomes. A father's mental wellness, parenting approach, and household setting are just a few examples of additional elements that can impact a child's growth and development.

The Dubbaca-jataka (Ja 116) offers a poignant lesson on the perils of alcohol. This tale recounts the tale of a Bodhisatta born into an acrobatic troupe. During a javelin dance lesson, a fellow acrobat imparts his wisdom to the Bodhisatta. This acrobat was a renowned performer who traveled the world, wowing audiences with his four-javelin dance. However, one fateful day, in a drunken stupor, he attempted the same dance with five javelins. Despite the Bodhisatta's warnings, the acrobat was too confident in his abilities and proceeded with the dangerous performance. Tragically, the Bodhisatta's warning proved true, and the acrobat perished after being impaled by the fifth javelin.

This narrative offers a clear message on the perils of alcohol that sets it apart from other stories. The protagonist's overconfidence and impaired judgment hindered his ability to heed the Bodhisatta's counsel, ultimately leading to his demise. It serves as a sobering reminder of how intoxication can have dire consequences. The media's comprehensive coverage of drunk driving incidents and overdoses underscores society's heightened awareness of the acute hazards associated with intoxication. According to empirical research, alcohol dependence is linked to an increased prevalence of high-risk behavior. A study conducted in India found that individuals who are dependent on alcohol are more likely to engage in dangerous behavior than those who are not (Korlakunta & Reddy, 2019). This research indicates that alcohol misuse not only poses a threat to the individual's well-being but can also endanger others. In addition, studies have shown a correlation between alcohol consumption and accidents resulting in injuries and fatalities (Cherpitel, 1999), much like the events described in this story. Specifically, road traffic accidents were the most common form of high-risk behavior observed. According to prior research, the consumption of alcohol is linked to hazardous and perilous driving habits (Donovan & Marlatt, 1982). While the conduct portrayed in the narrative is not aligned with these findings, they do corroborate the inference that the protagonist exhibited more reckless conduct while intoxicated compared to when sober.

The Gutha-Pana-jataka (Ja 227) portrays an interesting use of alcohol as a means of communication. The Bodhisatta, assuming the form of a tree fairy, observes the characters from a tree rather than playing a role in the story. According to the tale, travelers from two kingdoms would halt at a designated house during their journey and consume liquor and fish. A dung beetle was lured to the area by the scent of an ox's dung, hoping to find food. He stumbled upon a bottle of liquor on the ground and drank it all to quench his thirst, which left him thoroughly intoxicated. He then returned to a pile of dung and began to sink into it, calling out for help. At that moment, an elephant appeared but recoiled in disgust at the smell of the dung. A beetle challenged the elephant to a battle by crying out, confident that they were on equal footing. However, the elephant ignored the beetle and dropped a large piece of dung on it, killing it instantly. The moral of the story is that one should never overestimate their own power, as the wise elephant knew not to take on the confident beetle. Ultimately, the beetle paid the ultimate price for his hubris. The story's message serves as a valuable reminder to us all - despite our confidence, it is crucial to understand and respect our limitations, avoiding the pitfall of overestimating our abilities. Humility is key, and we must acknowledge when we are over our heads.

This tale offers a poignant metaphor for the perils of excessive drinking. Like the Dubbaca-jataka (Ja 116), its main aim seems to be to caution readers against the dangers of alcohol consumption. Studies carried out in India indicate that those who are dependent on alcohol are more prone to taking risks (Korlakunta & Reddy, 2019), a finding that has also been observed in Western populations. Moreover, research has linked alcohol use to heightened aggression, violent behavior, criminal activity, and decreased self-regulation (see Lane et al., 2004). Such actions can have negative consequences for one's mental health, social life, and overall well-being.

The Paniya-jataka (Ja 459) recounts the story of five Pacceka-Buddhas who gathered in Nandamula Cave after acquiring supernatural insight. One of these Pacceka-Buddhas was a wise landowner who had prohibited the sale of liquor in his kingdom. During their annual drinking festival, the people were troubled and approached him for guidance. The compassionate landowner permitted the festival to proceed as if liquor were legal, resulting in many drunken and violent individuals causing chaos. The intoxicated offenders were fined for their crimes, and the landowner felt remorse for his role in allowing the drinking to occur. Studies have shown that alcohol consumption is linked to violent and criminal behavior (Ensor & Godfrey, 1993; Milgram, 1993; Lanza-Kaduce et al., 1997). As a result of his remorse, the landowner developed supernatural insight and joined the other Pacceka-Buddhas in Nandamula Cave.

Before the main events of the story, the five Pacceka-Buddhas recount their asceticism to the king. The story reveals that one of the sins that led the landowner to become an ascetic was his allowance of others' transgressions while under the influence of alcohol. Other ascetics had histories of stealing, coveting women, and lying. Thus, it is clear from these examples of wrongdoing that consuming alcohol is not only a severe offense against oneself but also against others.

The story does not explicitly mention the allure of the forbidden fruit. Given that this festival is held annually, it can be assumed that the recent ban on alcohol occurred between the previous and current festivals, resulting in a period of deprivation for the attendees. Studies have demonstrated that simply forbidding something increases its appeal (Vingilis & de Genova, 1984). For instance, during the Vietnam War, the United States lowered the drinking age to 18, arguing that if young men were old enough to fight, they should also be allowed to drink (Douglass, 1979). However, permitting younger individuals to drink after years of prohibition proved challenging. Drunk driving accidents increased, and young people struggled to exercise self-control when it came to alcohol consumption. This ultimately led to the National Minimum Drinking Age Act being signed into law on July 17, 1984, raising the legal drinking age to 21 throughout the country.

The Maha-Sutasoma-jataka (Ja 537) highlights the risks associated with consuming alcohol at a young age, as well as the dangers of abstaining from it. Though the story primarily revolves around a greedy king's desire for human flesh, it also features several fables. Among these is the tale of a young boy who refuses to eat meat or drink alcohol. His peers try to pressure him into drinking by inviting him to a festival, assuring him that he can have milk instead. Despite their efforts, the boy remains steadfast in his decision. The men had hidden some liquor in a lotus leaf and asked the young boy to fetch them some lotus nectar. The boy innocently consumed the liquor, mistaking it for nectar. As he continued to drink more, the men offered him meat, which he happily ate. Eventually, the boy became highly intoxicated, unaware that he was drinking liquor and not nectar.

Despite the deception, the boy did not seem to care and continued to request more liquor. He was thoroughly enjoying the taste and spent the entire day drinking with the men. When he finally returned home, he fell asleep. However, his father soon discovered what had happened and scolded him, warning him never to drink again.

The young man failed to grasp the gravity of his actions, as the taste of liquor was too alluring. When he expressed his unwillingness to give up drinking to his father, the latter warned him that their family's fortune and reputation would suffer if he continued. Despite his father's objections, the son remained steadfast in his refusal to quit. Eventually, he ended up homeless and destitute in the city until his passing. This cautionary tale serves as a reminder to the king about the dangers of uncontrolled desire and the need to refrain from consuming human flesh.

A poignant tale recounts the story of a father who was deeply concerned about the welfare of his son and went to great lengths to avoid enabling him. Enabling is defined as the act of facilitating the avoidance of negative consequences resulting from an alcoholic's behavior (Koppel et al., 1980). While this behavior usually carries a negative connotation, it was a loving gesture of support from a father to his son in this particular instance. To illustrate enabling an alcoholic, one could offer to purchase more alcohol for them when they are low on cash, bail them out of jail if they are detained for alcohol-related offenses, make excuses for them when they miss work or other commitments due to alcohol use, and so on. In this story, the father plays an antagonist to the enabler, allowing his son to face the harsh realities and negative consequences of his drinking. Interestingly, the Bodhisatta, Sakka, provides a clear example of an enabler in the Bhadra-Ghata-jataka (Ja 291).

This narrative serves as a compelling example of how society communicates the hazards of alcohol consumption. Through the account of a young boy who falls prey to addiction after consuming alcohol and human flesh, the story employs the vices of the king as allegories. The widespread use of this messaging underscores the negative stereotypes that can come with alcohol misuse. The consumption of alcohol beyond legal limits can have grave consequences, and this story effectively cautions readers about its dangers. By emphasizing the need to limit alcohol intake, this story serves as a powerful tool for promoting responsible drinking.

Stigma of Alcoholism

Alcohol addiction, along with other forms of addiction, is often stigmatized due to societal factors (Schomerus et al., 2005). This can be attributed to the negative associations that come with alcohol abuse, including health risks and the potential for violence, which are frequently highlighted in the media. Furthermore, alcohol is often tied to strong moral and religious values, leading to further judgment and discrimination. Unfortunately, people may overlook the fact that alcohol addiction is a disease, instead attributing personal blame to those who are struggling with it. This can result in stigma and prejudice, making it more challenging for individuals with alcohol addiction to seek the necessary support and treatment to recover. After all, one would not blame an individual for developing cancer, so why should we blame someone for developing an addiction?

Studies reveal that individuals battling addiction tend to assign more blame, experience more negative emotions, and are less likely to assist cancer patients (Switzer & Boysen, 2009). Furthermore, it is evident that negative attitudes toward alcohol addiction have remained unchanged since 1990, despite extensive research on its causes and categorization as a mental illness (Schomerus et al., 2014). This underscores the importance of increased public awareness and resources devoted to mental health services. Education and support are crucial in reducing the stigma and enhancing comprehension of addiction.

In the above discussions, we delve into the portrayal of alcohol in Buddhist texts and explore the connection between religiosity and negative attitudes towards individuals with addiction. It is believed that religious teachings, which discourage alcohol consumption, may contribute to the stigma surrounding drug use. However, studies on the correlation between religion and stigmatizing attitudes have yielded conflicting results (Switzer & Boysen, 2009). This indicates that the relationship between religious teachings and people's perception of substance abuse is multifaceted. Although religious teachings may discourage the consumption of alcohol, research suggests that it does not necessarily lead to greater stigmatization of those struggling with addiction.

Substance Abuse: Coping Mechanisms and Moral Lessons

In the upcoming section, we will delve into several Jataka stories that explore the negative connotations surrounding alcohol consumption. Although the characters in these stories do not necessarily center around alcohol, it is often used to create an overall negative association. One such tale is Varuni-jataka (Ja 47), which follows the Bodhisatta when he was a treasurer. In this short story, an apprentice left in charge of a tavern mistakenly ruined all the liquor by salting it, resulting in unhappy customers. The tavern-keeper then explained to the Bodhisatta that those who attempt to do good without the proper knowledge can often cause harm instead.

While this story does not seem to directly relate to alcohol, it does subtly suggest that the owner of a bar endures losses in the end. It might be assumed that the tavern keeper's misfortune was caused by the sale and consumption of alcohol. However, research shows that bartenders, including those who own and manage bars like the one in this story, are actually very likely to intervene when they see a patron drinking excessively (Zafer et al., 2018). Therefore, it is not necessarily accurate to assume that a bartender or bar owner approves of irresponsible drinking habits.

The Punnapati-jataka (Ja 53) does not make any direct mention of alcohol but rather depicts the Bodhisatta as Treasurer in a past life. A group of men approach him and invite him to share some fine liquor, but the Bodhisatta, who abstains from alcohol, is wary of their request. Instead of simply declining, he promises to consult with the king first. Upon his return, he notices that none of the men have consumed any liquor. The Bodhisatta then reveals that the men attempted to poison and rob him by spiking the liquor, as he was the city's treasurer. He points out that if the liquor had truly been of high quality, the men would have consumed some while they waited for his return.

Compared to Varuni-jataka (Ja 47), the consumption of alcohol is not pivotal to the main message conveyed in the story. In reality, the men's alcohol consumption proved to be a hindrance as the Bodhisatta did not partake in it due to his religious and ethical beliefs. It is plausible that these men had attempted a similar tactic on previous Treasurers and were unaware of the Bodhisatta's abstention from alcohol. All things considered, the men would have had greater success in poisoning the Bodhisatta had they utilized drugged tea or soup instead.

Similar to the preceding account, it seems that the primary function of alcohol in the Bodhisatta's tales is to establish an unfavorable perception of those who endeavor to deceive him. Multiple investigations have suggested that alcohol dependence is linked with negative outlooks and actions (Schomerus et al., 2014). Consequently, it is reasonable why an adverse association with alcohol gradually develops as a consequence of traditional stories like those recounted in the jataka stories. Given that these narratives are transmitted from one generation to the next, it can prove challenging to reverse the psychological associations and attributions that are tied to alcohol.

The Surapana-jataka (Ja 81) recounts the tale of the Bodhisatta's previous existence as a Brahmin adult who embraced the solitary lifestyle of a hermit. A group of 500 Himalayan hermits, known for their exceptional moral character, had taken up residence in the king's garden. In a generous act of kindness, the king permitted them to stay for a period of four months.

Substance Abuse: Coping Mechanisms and Moral Lessons

In the city, a drinking festival was held, and the king generously provided 500 hermits with a considerable amount of premium liquor. As hermits have chosen to forgo worldly pleasures, they seldom get the chance to indulge in such exquisite spirits. After consuming the liquor, the hermits returned to their abode in the garden. Some attendees danced, and others sang, having become inebriated. The next morning, upon recollecting their actions from the previous night, they were filled with remorse and shame. They claim that due to their prolonged separation from their master, they were vulnerable to temptation and left the royal garden for the Himalayas.

Upon returning home, their master inquired about their stay. Admitting to imbibing the forbidden drink, they vowed to refrain from doing so in the future. This resonates with the teachings of the Paniya-jataka (Ja 459), which also forbids alcohol. The allure of something forbidden can make it more appealing, as noted by Vingilis and de Genova (1984). Abstaining from alcohol may have exacerbated their drinking habits, as they were unaware of how to regulate their intake. As a result, they became excessively intoxicated, leading to shame over their actions. It is worth noting that alcohol can be consumed in moderation without reaching a state of intoxication. It is intriguing to consider how the hermits would have approached alcohol had they learned to consume it moderately.

The narrative highlights the hermits' sense of shame upon regaining sobriety, which is a unique aspect compared to other accounts. Studies have revealed that negative emotions like guilt, shame, dread, anger, and regret can be induced when one experiences an alcohol hangover (Milton et al., 2020). This is because alcohol can impede emotional regulation, leading to heightened emotional responses during a hungover state. There are several factors that can contribute to negative emotions when consuming alcohol, such as the social and cultural context in which it is consumed, as well as the biochemical effects it has on the brain (as discussed in Milton et al., 2020). Specifically, those living in cultures where alcohol use is stigmatized may be more prone to experiencing negative emotions after excessive drinking. For instance, individuals in certain Asian countries where alcohol consumption is discouraged often report feelings of guilt and shame following drinking, as compared to those in countries where alcohol consumption is more accepted.

Additionally, when alcohol is consumed, it releases "happy" neurotransmitters like serotonin, which accounts for the general sense of euphoria often linked with drinking (Lovinger, 1997). However, these same neurotransmitters are soon depleted, resulting in a crash that can cause feelings of anxiety and depression. This can lead to a heightened desire for alcohol, setting in motion a dangerous cycle that may ultimately result in addiction. As a depressant, alcohol gradually lowers serotonin levels, leading to depression or depression-related conditions. Therefore, it appears that alcohol can contribute to negative emotions even when consumed in a social context.

This particular tale is unique in its depiction of both the emotional and physical aftermath of excessive alcohol consumption. Interestingly, none of the Jataka tales touch upon the latter. It is possible that this is because the impact of alcohol on one's emotions and behavior is deemed more significant than the physical discomfort that follows. Regrettably, the physical aspect of alcohol use is frequently disregarded, even in literature. This narrative, however, is a noteworthy exception, delving deeply into the bodily effects of alcohol. It is a valuable reminder of the potential repercussions that can arise from overindulgence.

The Sigala-jataka (Ja 113) recounts a tale of the Bodhisatta, who was a tree spirit residing in a cemetery. During a town festival, the people gathered a considerable quantity of fish and meat, along with liquor, for the celebration. While the town was asleep, a jackal crept in through the sewers and indulged in the feast. After falling asleep in some bushes, he could not wake up until the next morning. Realizing that he could not leave the city on his own, the jackal resorted to tricking a Brahmin into helping him.

This narrative shares a common theme of the jackal's deceitfulness. However, unlike other tales, the Bodhisatta does not use it as a chance to impart a profound moral lesson. Rather, the Bodhisatta kindly rebukes the Brahmin for being deceived by the inebriated jackal. It is possible that the jackal was meant to be portrayed as an immoral figure, where stealing meat could be seen as just as wrong as stealing alcohol. The message seems to focus not solely on alcohol but, more broadly, on the concept of dishonesty as a whole. In this story, portraying an animal as the main character who drinks alcohol may be seen as dehumanizing by those who struggle with alcohol addiction. It is important to differentiate between dehumanization and stigmatization - the former entails stripping someone of their innate humanity, including qualities like civility, moral sensibility, and interpersonal warmth (Haslam, 2006). This can take many forms, from denying basic rights to treating someone as subhuman or objectifying them. Ultimately, dehumanization undermines an individual's inherent worth and dignity, and it is often used to justify mistreatment, discrimination, and violence.

According to Haslam (2006), one way people dehumanize others is by comparing them to nonhuman animals or referring to them as such. For instance, the phrase "men are dogs" is a dehumanizing statement that is often used to justify why men can be sexually aggressive, making it easier to punish them. Other phrases that refer to individuals as "rats" or "pigs" also exist. As such, when we use examples of dishonest jackals who enjoy gluttony, we effectively dehumanize people who share such traits. This kind of language strips individuals of their humanity and normalizes negative behaviors. Therefore, it is crucial to be aware of the implications of such language and avoid using it.

Studies indicate that depicting an immoral character as an animal may dehumanize those struggling with alcohol addiction and make it harder for them to seek treatment (Schomerus et al., 2011). Alcohol dependence often leads to self-dehumanization, which results in feelings of anxiety, depression, and decreased self-worth. Despite widespread awareness of the dangers of alcoholism and addiction, the stigma attached to these issues can prevent individuals from seeking help. Fear of judgment and rejection can exacerbate these feelings of dehumanization, creating a cycle that is difficult to break.

In contrast to the other tales featured in this chapter, the Bodhisatta takes the form of a jackal in the Sigala-jataka (Ja 142). This particular jataka bears a resemblance to the Sigala-jataka (Ja 113). During a lively celebration in the city, a group of men indulged in an abundance of food and drink, singing and reveling into the night. As the midnight hour approached, the meat supply dwindled. One of the men then ventured into a nearby grove in search of jackals, hoping to secure more meat for the festivities.

A man ventured into the sewers and feigned death, waiting for a jackal to appear. The Bodhisatta, disguised as a jackal, came upon the scene and inspected the motionless body. He quickly recognized the ruse by the scent and decided to play a prank on the man. The Bodhisatta pretended to take the man's club, causing the man to tighten his hold on it, unaware of the trick being played on him. The Bodhisatta then revealed the truth to the man.

It is worth noting that the message of the story could still be communicated without the presence of alcohol. While it is not explicitly stated in the narrative, it is possible that the man was intoxicated when he made the foolish decision to hunt for jackals at night. Studies have established a link between alcohol consumption and risky behavior (Halpern-Felsher et al., 1996; Testa & Collins, 1997), which underscores the potential connection between alcohol use and recklessness.

One notable contrast between this tale and its predecessor lies in the Bodhisatta's current form as a jackal. This is a common theme in jataka stories, which often portray the Bodhisatta as an animal in a past life. Despite his nonhuman appearance, he is revered for his virtuous nature and often exhibits human-like traits that allow him to outsmart his foes. As a result, he stands out as a compelling and inspirational figure in Buddhist literature.

In the Dhammaddhaja-jataka (Ja 220), it is recounted that the Bodhisatta was challenged to create a man with four virtues but claimed it was impossible. However, Sakka directed him to a man named Chattapani, who possessed all four virtues. When asked about his virtues, Chattapani revealed that he abstained from drinking any wine or alcohol due to a past experience where he consumed alcohol and ate the flesh of his own son while intoxicated. According to Chattapani, alcohol was the root cause of this terrible event, which led him to never drink alcohol again.

While some stories may suggest that excessive alcohol consumption can lead to extreme consequences, such as cannibalism, there is no evidence to support this claim in modern or earlier research. Studies have shown a link between alcohol consumption and disinhibited eating, which can lead to reckless and dangerous behavior (Kane et al., 2004). However, spontaneous cannibalism is not mentioned in these studies. Nevertheless, research on rats suggests that alcohol can increase the likelihood of dangerous behavior, such as cannibalism (Abel, 1979). It is crucial to always exercise caution and be aware of the potential hazards associated with consuming alcohol.

The Nana-Cchanda-jataka (Ja 289) portrays thieves drinking and carrying liquor while assaulting the disguised king (who was the Bodhisatta in a past life). Although alcohol is not a primary focus, it represents the characters' immorality and wrongdoing. This aligns with Buddhist principles that discourage excess and overindulgence. Generally, the story depicts alcohol as a substance that can lead to criminal behavior, which should be avoided.

According to research by Lane et al. (2004), there is a link between alcohol consumption and an increased tendency towards criminal activity. However, it is important to note that not all individuals who consume alcohol will automatically become criminals. Alcohol addiction is a complex issue that involves a multitude of social, individual, and biological factors, which need to be evaluated on a case-by-case basis. While excessive alcohol consumption may be a contributing factor to criminal behavior, it is not the only one. Other factors such as genetics, upbringing, and social environment can also play a role in an individual's propensity to commit crimes.

Enabling Alcoholism

As mentioned earlier in this chapter, the Bhadra-Ghata-jataka (Ja 291) showcases the perils of enabling in the context of alcoholism recovery. The tale narrates the story of a Bodhisatta who is reborn as the son of a wealthy merchant, leaving behind a legacy for future generations. After his father's demise, he takes over the family business and has one son. Throughout his life, he leads a virtuous life as a merchant, and after his death, he is reborn as Sakka. However, his son lives a non-virtuous life and spends most of his time drinking, singing, and dancing with his friends. His irresponsible behavior leads him to squander all his wealth quickly, and he becomes destitute. When Sakka realizes his son's predicament, he descends to earth and gifts him a wishing cup. He assures his son that he would never face poverty as long as he possesses the cup.

Unfortunately, the son only indulged in drinking from the cup. One fateful day, he imbibed to the point of becoming intoxicated and began playing a game of throwing the cup up in the air and catching it. Tragically, he missed his catch, and the cup shattered on the ground. This unfortunate incident led to a lifetime of destitution, where he resorted to begging and ultimately met his demise.

Similarly to the preceding narrative, it seems that alcohol is linked with detrimental lifestyle patterns rather than being intrinsically harmful. Apart from consuming alcohol, the son squandered all his earnings on food and additional alcohol. It is possible that his perpetual inebriation impeded his discernment to such an extent that he made these other regrettable decisions. Additionally, the son failed to acquire any substantial trade expertise throughout his lifetime, which meant that after the wishing cup was shattered, he had no source of income.

A noteworthy element that distinguishes this story from others is the role played by Sakka, the Bodhisatta, as an enabler. Rather than compelling the son to quit drinking, Sakka gratifies his thirst for alcohol out of affection, which ultimately deepens the son's dependence on it, exacerbating the entire scenario. This situation exemplifies enabling behavior. Sakka's love and concern for his son is evident in his decision to satisfy his son's craving for alcohol instead of helping him overcome it. Unfortunately, this allowed his son's alcoholism to persist and even worsen. Sakka's actions serve as a cautionary tale about how enabling someone's negative behavior can have long-term consequences. Studies show that the presence of an enabler, someone who is not addicted but provides assistance and support to the addicted individual, can significantly impede the addict's ability to recover from alcohol addiction (Miller & Millman, 1989). Many alcoholics rely on an enabler to sustain their drinking habits, even without the involvement of a clinician or therapist. For example, alcohol is an expensive substance, and alcoholics may find themselves without the funds to purchase it. Without an enabler, a person might be forced to steal alcohol or quit drinking altogether.

While the wishing cup is just one instance of empowerment in this situation, it is worth noting that the Bodhisatta also devoted his life to instructing his son on how to be a merchant.

Conclusion

Alcohol use and addiction are multifaceted and intricate issues that have affected human beings for centuries. Even nonhuman animals have been known to exhibit behaviors suggesting the consumption of alcohol. Despite the growing awareness of the negative effects of alcohol, we have not seen a significant increase in the number of people abstaining from alcohol consumption and indulgence. This suggests that the reasons behind why individuals choose to drink and continue to drink may be more complex than just the desire for health and well-being. There may be deeper motivations at play, such as psychological or social factors, that contribute to a person's relationship with alcohol.

Given the long-standing and ongoing struggles that humans face with alcohol, it is crucial to prioritize effective treatment methods and societal acceptance of addiction. Research has shown that addiction is not always given the same weight as other mental disorders, highlighting the need for a shift away from negative judgment and towards the development of therapies for alcoholism (Schomerus et al., 2011).

Unfortunately, the stigma surrounding addiction often prevents individuals from seeking the help they need. Not only can it be difficult to admit to a problem that is so often demonized, but individuals also face societal stigmatization of mental health care in general (Owen et al., 2013). This harmful stereotype portrays addicts as weak-willed, irresponsible, and morally corrupt. This can significantly impact an individual's ability to seek help. As a result, many individuals are hesitant to speak openly about their addiction, and even those who do may not receive the assistance they require.

As a society, we need to shift our perception of addiction. It is unfair to imply that individuals struggling with alcohol dependence are somehow weaker or more responsible for their condition than those dealing with cancer or other mental health disorders. In fact, the treatment plans and lifestyle changes required for alcohol addiction are often far more demanding than those for diabetes or hypertension (McLellan et al., 2000). Those battling alcohol addiction face the realities of their disease every moment of every day during treatment. Despite being subjected to the same responsibilities and pressures that drove them to drink in the first place, they must find new coping mechanisms. It takes a strong and determined individual to successfully follow such a rigorous treatment plan.

Addiction is an incredibly intricate issue that impacts millions of people globally. It is a complex disease that can be triggered by a variety of factors and can present itself in many different forms, making it challenging to manage effectively. Understanding the intricacies of this issue and its profound impact on individuals and society is crucial.

Alcohol addiction is a complex issue that requires attention to several interrelated factors. Among these are the harmful effects of excessive consumption and the stigma that often surrounds addiction to alcohol. These challenges can discourage people from seeking assistance and make the situation more complex, potentially leading to additional problems.

The role of a supportive figure in an alcoholic's recovery journey is crucial. Such a person can either enable the addiction or aid the individual in their efforts to overcome it. This emphasizes the significance of having a robust support system in place. It can serve as a determining factor in an individual's path to recovery.

The accounts of those who have triumphed over alcohol addiction offer a window into the psychological and emotional challenges that individuals confront when on the path to recovery. These challenges may involve experiencing emotions such as shame, guilt, and anxiety, among others. It is essential to interact with individuals in a compassionate and considerate manner as they strive towards a healthier existence and a brighter tomorrow.

In essence, these narratives provide hope and motivation to individuals who are grappling with addiction, underscoring that healing is attainable and a better future is within reach. Moreover, they underscore the significance of spreading awareness about addiction and extending assistance to those in need.

References

Abel, E. L. (1979). Effects of alcohol withdrawal and undernutrition on cannibalism of rat pups. *Behavioral and Neural Biology*, 25(3), 411-413.https://doi.org/10.1016/S0163-1047(79)91320-4

American Psychiatric Association. (2013). *Diagnostic and statistical manual of mental disorders* (5th ed.). American Psychiatric Publishing.

Benegal, V., Velayudan, A., & Jain, S. (2000). The social costs of alcoholism (Karnataka). *NIMHANS Journal*, 18, 67–76.

Bonu, S., Rani, M., Peters, D. H., Jha, P., & Nguyem, S. N. (2005). Does use of tobacco or alcohol contribute to impoverishment from hospitalization costs in India? *Health Policy and Planning*, 20(1), 41–49. https://doi.org/10.1093/heapol/czi005

Cherpitel, C. J. (1999). Substance use, injury, and risk-taking disposition in the general population. *Alcoholism: Clinical and Experimental Research*, 23(1), 121–126. https://doi.org/10.1111/j.1530-0277.1999.tb04031.x

Donovan, D. M., & Marlatt, G. A. (1982). Personality subtypes among driving-while-intoxicated offenders: Relationship to drinking behavior and driving task. *Journal of Consulting and Clinical Psychology*, 50(2), 241–249. https://doi.org/10.1037/0022-006X.50.2.241

Douglass, R. L. (1979). The legal drinking age and traffic casualties: A special case of changing alcohol availability in a public health context. *Alcohol Health and Research World*, 4(2), 18-25.

Eashwar, V., Umadevi, R., & Gopalakrishnan, S. (2020). Alcohol consumption in India - An epidemiological review. *Journal of Family Medicine and Primary Care*, 9(1), 49–55. https://doi.org/10.4103/jfmpc.jfmpc_575_19

Ensor, T., & Godfrey, C. (1993). Modelling the interactions between alcohol, crime and the criminal justice system. *Addiction*, 88(4), 477–487. https://doi.org/10.1111/j.1360-0443.1993.tb00834.x

Ferguson, E., Fiore, A., Yurasek, A. M., Cook, R. L., & Boissoneault, J. (2022). Association of therapeutic and recreational reasons for alcohol use with alcohol demand. *Experimental and Clinical Psychopharmacology*. Advance online publication. https://doi.org/10.1037/pha0000568

Fontesse, S., Demoulin, S., Stinglhamber, F., de Timary, P., & Maurage, P. (2021). Metadehumanization and self-dehumanization are linked to reduced drinking refusal self-efficacy and increased anxiety and depression symptoms in patients with severe alcohol use disorder. *Psychologica Belgica*, 61(1), 238–247. https://doi.org/10.5334/pb.1078

Halpern-Felsher, B. L., Millstein, S. G., & Ellen, J. M. (1996). Relationship of alcohol use and risky sexual behavior: A review and analysis of findings. *Journal of Adolescent Health*, 19(5), 331–336. https://doi.org/10.1016/S1054-139X(96)00165-5

Haslam, N. (2006). Dehumanization: *An integrative review*. *Personality and Social Psychology Review*, 10(3), 252–264. https://doi.org/10.1207/s15327957pspr1003_4

Kane, T. A., Loxton, N. J., Staiger, P. K., & Dawe, S. (2004). Does the tendency to act impulsively underlie binge eating and alcohol use problems? An empirical investigation. *Personality and Individual Differences*, 36(1), 83-94. https://doi.org/10.1016/S0191-8869(03)00070-9

Koppel, F., Stimmler, L., & Perone, F. (1980). The enabler: A motivational tool in treating the alcoholic. *Social Casework*, 61(9), 577–583. https://doi.org/10.1177/104438948006100904

Korlakunta, A., & Reddy, C. P. (2019). High-risk behavior in patients with alcohol dependence. *Indian Journal of Psychiatry*, 61(1), 125. https://doi.org/10.4103/psychiatry.IndianJPsychiatry_140_18

Lane, S. D., Cherek, D. R., Pietras, C. J., & Tcheremissine, O. V. (2004). Alcohol effects on human risk-taking. *Psychopharmacology*, 172(1), 68-77. https://doi.org/10.1007/s00213-003-1620-2

Lanza-Kaduce, L., Bishop, D. M., & Winner, L. (1997). Risk/benefit calculations, moral evaluations, and alcohol use: Exploring the alcohol-crime connection. *Crime & Delinquency*, 43(2), 222–239. https://doi.org/10.1177/0011128797043002006

Lovinger, D. M. (1997). Serotonin's role in alcohol's effects on the brain. *Alcohol Health and Research World*, 21(2), 114-120.

McLellan, A. T., Lewis, D. C., O'Brien, C. P., & Kleber, H. D. (2000). Drug dependence, a chronic medical illness: Implications for treatment, insurance, and outcomes evaluation. *Journal of the American Medical Association*, 284(13), 1689-1695. https://doi.org/10.1001/jama.284.13.1689

Milgram, G. G. (1993). Adolescents, alcohol and aggression. *Journal of Studies on Alcohol and Drugs Supplement*, 11, 53–56. https://doi.org/10.15288/jsas.1993.s11.53

Miller, N. S., & Millman, R. B. (1989). A common cause of alcoholism. *Journal of Substance Abuse Treatment*, 6(1), 41-43. https://doi.org/10.1016/0740-5472(89)90055-2

Milton, I. J., Sillence, E., & Mitchell, M. (2020). Exploring the emotional experiences of alcohol hangover syndrome in healthy UK-based adults. *Drugs: Education, Prevention and Policy*, 27(3), 248-260. https://doi.org/10.1080/09687637.2019.1622311

Nelson, M. C., Lust, K., Story, M., & Ehlinger, E. (2009). Alcohol use, eating patterns, and weight behaviors in a university population. *American Journal of Health Behavior*, 33(3), 227-237. https://doi.org/10.5993/AJHB.33.3.2

Owen, J., Thomas, L., & Rodolfa, E. (2013). Stigma for seeking therapy: Self-stigma, social stigma, and therapeutic processes. *The Counseling Psychologist*, 41(6), 857-880. https://doi.org/10.1177/0011000012459365

Pihl, R. O., Peterson, J., & Finn, P. R. (1990). Inherited predisposition to alcoholism: Characteristics of sons of male alcoholics. *Journal of Abnormal Psychology*, 99(3), 291–301. https://doi.org/10.1037/0021-843X.99.3.291

Schomerus, G., Lucht, M., Holzinger, A., Matschinger, H., Carta, M. G., & Angermeyer, M. C. (2011). The stigma of alcohol dependence compared with other mental disorders: A review of population studies. *Alcohol and Alcoholism*, 46(2), 105–112. https://doi.org/10.1093/alcalc/agq089

Schomerus, G., Matschinger, H., & Angermeyer, M. C. (2005). Alcoholism: Illness beliefs and resource allocation preference of the public. *Drug and Alcohol Dependence*, 82(3), 204–210. https://doi.org/10.1016/j.drugalcdep.2005.08.008

Schomerus, G., Matschinger, H., & Angermeyer, M. C. (2014). Attitudes towards alcohol dependence and affected individuals: Persistence of negative stereotypes and illness beliefs between 1990 and 2011. *European Addiction Research*, 20(6), 293-299. https://doi.org/10.1159/000367940

Singh, A. K. (2020). Drug (intoxicant) addiction and Buddhism: Problems and remedies. *Sri Lanka International Journal of Buddhist Studies*, 6, 8-22.

Switzer, B., & Boysen, G. A. (2009). The impact of religiosity and attribution theory on attitudes toward addiction and cancer. *Mental Health, Religion & Culture*, 12(3), 241-245. https://doi.org/10.1080/13674670902758257

Testa, M., & Collins, R. L. (1997). Alcohol and risky sexual behavior: Event-based analyses among a sample of high-risk women. *Psychology of Addictive Behaviors*, 11(3), 190-201. https://doi.org/10.1037/0893-164X.11.3.190

Vingilis, E. R., & De Genova, K. (1984). Youth and the forbidden fruit: Experiences with changes in legal drinking age in North America. *Journal of Criminal Justice*, 12(2), 161-172. https://doi.org/10.1016/0047-2352(84)90014-4

Volkow, N. D., Koob, G. F., & McLellan, A. T. (2016). Neurobiologic advances from the brain disease model of addiction. *The New England Journal of Medicine*, 374(4), 363-371. https://doi.org/10.1056/NEJMra1511480

World Health Organization. (2004). *Global status report on alcohol*. World Health Organization.

World Health Organization. (2018). *Global status report on alcohol and health 2018*. https://www.who.int/publications/i/item/9789241565639

World Health Organization. (2018). *Alcohol*. https://www.who.int/en/news-room/fact-sheets/detail/alcohol

Zafer, M., Liu, S., & Katz, C. L. (2018). Bartenders' and rum shopkeepers' knowledge of and attitudes toward "problem drinking" in Saint Vincent and the Grenadines. *Psychiatric Quarterly*, 89(4), 801–815. https://doi.org/10.1007/s11126-018-9587-7

Further Recommended Readings

Appleton, N., & Shaw, S. (Trans.). (2015). *The ten great birth stories of the Bodhisatta*. Silkworm Press.

Cowell, E. B., & Neil, R. A. (Eds.). (1895–1907). *The Jātaka or stories of the Buddha's former births* (6 vols.). Cambridge University Press.

Sumanacara, A. (2024). *The tale of Prince Vessantara: A novel*. Subhashita Books.

About the Author

Ashin Sumanacara holds a Ph.D. in Buddhist Studies from Mahidol University and an MA from the University of Kelaniya. His academic focus is on the psychological and philosophical aspects of Buddhist teachings, particularly through the study of the Pali suttas and Jataka stories.

In addition to his scholarly work, Ashin Sumanacara has practiced meditation in Myanmar and Thailand under the guidance of renowned meditation masters. His experiences with mindfulness and insight meditation inform his role as a spiritual counselor, where he integrates mindfulness-based cognitive-behavioral therapy into his practice, supporting individuals on their path to well-being.

He is also the author of *'Meaningful Life, Fearless Death: Spiritual Insights on Death, Dying, and Hospice Care'* (2022) and *'The Tale of Prince Vessantara: A Novel'* (2024), reflecting his dedication to exploring Buddhist teachings in both academic and narrative forms. Ashin Sumanacara's work reflects his commitment to both academic study and practical spiritual application, aimed at fostering personal growth and mindfulness.

PUBLISHED BOOKS

By
Ashin Sumanacara

Meaningful Life, Fearless Death
Spiritual Insights on Death, Dying, Hospice Care and Grief Counseling

The Tale Of Prince Vessantara
A Novel

The Bodhisatta's Wisdom
Illustrated Jataka Fables of Animals

SUBHASHITA BOOKS

SUBHASHITA BOOKS publishes a diverse range of insightful literature that explores Eastern philosophy, self-help, mindfulness and spiritual teachings

SUBHASHITA BOOKS

3381 Boul Dagenais O.

Laval, QC, Canada

H7P IV5

Subhashita Books is affiliated with a non-profit organization and distributes published books and educational resources.

www.ingramcontent.com/pod-product-compliance
Lightning Source LLC
Chambersburg PA
CBHW060558080526
44585CB00013B/614